EXPLORER
BUGS!

By **Nick Forshaw** & **William Exley**

?

What on Earth Publishing Ltd., The Black Barn, Wickhurst Farm, Tonbridge, Kent TN11 8PS, United Kingdom

First published in 2018.

© What on Earth Publishing Ltd., 2018.

All rights reserved. No part of this publication may be reproduced or transmitted in any form or by any means, electronic or mechanical, including photocopying, recording, or any information storage or retrieval system, without permission in writing from the publishers. Requests for permission to make copies of any part of this work should be directed to info@whatonearthbooks.com.

Produced in association with the Natural History Museum, London.

Written by Nicholas Forshaw, Patrick Skipworth and Christopher Lloyd.
Illustrated by William Exley.
Designed by Andy Forshaw and Assunção Sampayo.

ISBN: 978-0-9955766-0-5

Printed by Waiman in China.

10 9 8 7 6 5 4 3 2 1

whatonearthbooks.com

CONTENTS

AGENT ASSIGNED: Agent Eagle

YOUR MISSION: Calling Agent Eagle! You must once again venture into the unknown. Explorer HQ need a report on bugs ASAP! Go out and explore every creepy crawly you can find.

1. WHAT IS A BUG?

6

2. BUG BEGINNINGS

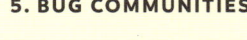

10

3. GIANT BUGS

14

4. BUG LIFE

18

5. BUG COMMUNITIES

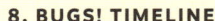

22

6. BUGS AND HUMANS

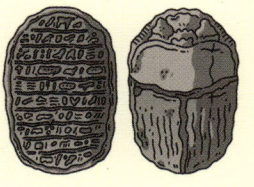

26

7. PLANET OF THE BUGS

30

8. BUGS! TIMELINE

AGENT EAGLE

I'm Eric Eagle, Senior Librarian of the Eagle-Eyed Explorer Club. Years ago, the club recruited me as one of its special agents – codename, Agent Eagle.

Most days you'll find me in the basement of the library, organising the atlases. But I always keep my rucksack at the ready, in case the club needs me for one of its urgent missions. I never know when to expect a call.

STAFF ROOM ←
LIBRARY ←
BUGS! →

Mission Checklist

1x Explorer Field Notebook
1x Magnifying Glass
1x Binoculars
1x Agent Issue Torch
1x Portable Time Machine
1x Sandwich (cheese & pickle)

My latest mission is not only top secret, but very dangerous, so keep it hush-hush. The club has ordered me to file a report on the entire history of bugs as soon as possible. It looks like I'll need to go back millions of years in time.

I'll need to fill out a Journal to keep track of my discoveries. I'm also drawing up a Timeline to show the life story of bugs, from the ancient seas to the present day.

No time to waste. Are you feeling brave? Let's go!

1. WHAT IS A BUG?

OPABINIA

'Way, way back in time, before the dinosaurs, before the woolly mammoths, long before human beings, some ancient forms of life were swimming through the oceans that covered planet Earth. Five hundred and forty million years ago, these creatures began to change rapidly into new and different forms, in an evolutionary explosion that altered life on Earth entirely. Their descendants still exist all over the world today, in every continent and every country, in every crevice and every corner, creatures we call ... bugs!'

On the Origin of (Bug) Species

In the Cambrian period 540 million years ago, the ancestors of today's bugs were spread out through the oceans, where seaweed streamed in the currents and green blobs of algae slopped around in the waves. Sea sponges clung to the rocks in the shallows. Trilobites swam through the seas in their thousands, their compact bodies helping them survive. These creatures were early types of arthropod, a group of bugs that includes many species today. Scientists call this time the 'Cambrian Explosion', as countless numbers of creatures evolved all at once and continued to flourish in the following Ordovician period too.

Hallucigenia – wrong way up!

Opabinia was a five-eyed, prong-headed predator that hunted through coral reefs for ancient fish-like species to eat, gobbling up its prey on the seafloor. *Ramphoprion* had a strange angular body, but is a distant relative of the modern earthworm. Two-metre-long *Aegirocassis* swam with its jaws wide open, scooping tiny marine organisms into its mouth. Explorers first thought the spikes on *Hallucigenia*'s back were its legs, although they were mystified as to how this underwater creature could move on such pointy sticks. The mystery was cleared up when scientists pointed out that it had been reconstructed upside down. Oops!

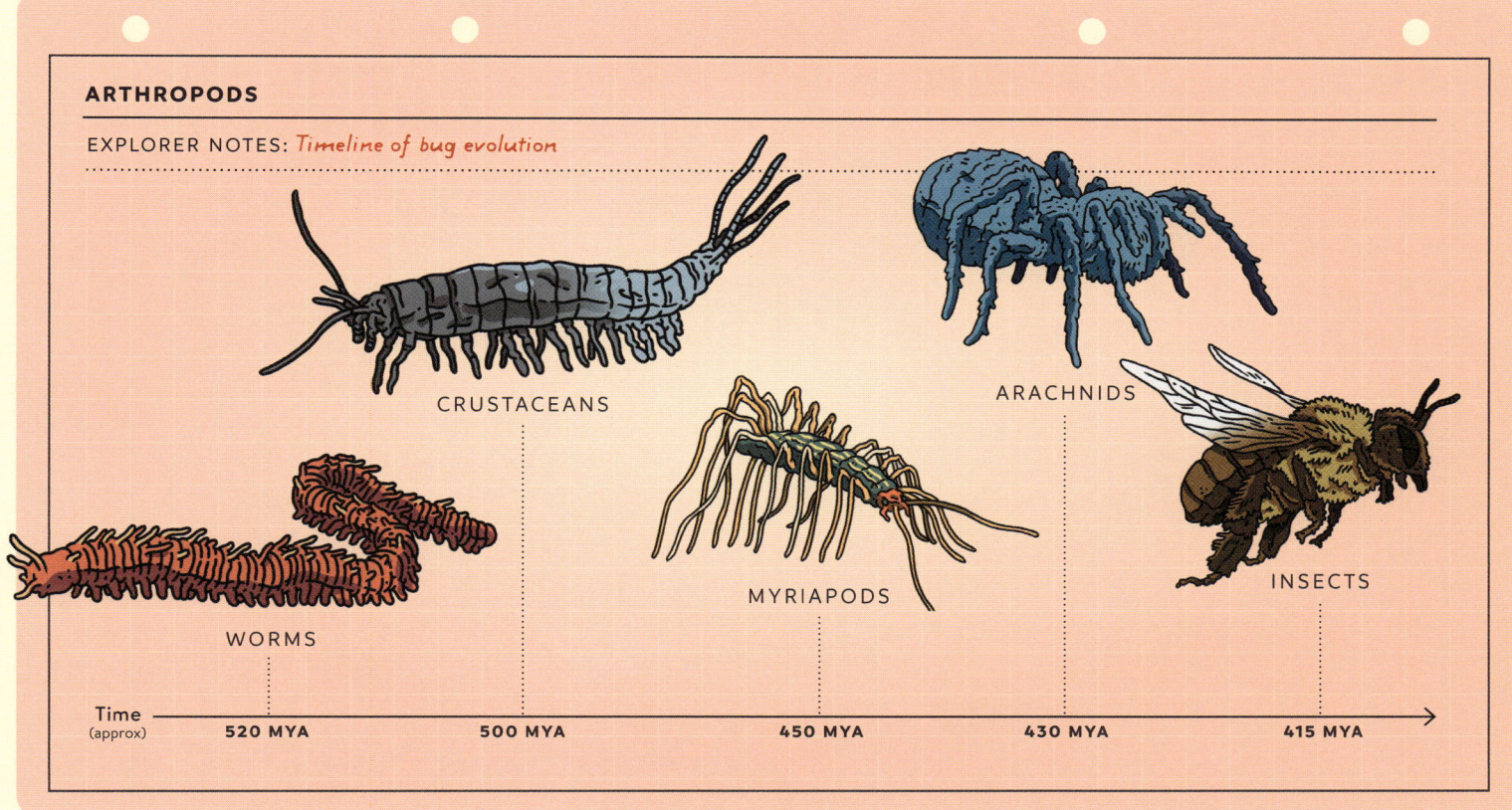

ARTHROPODS

EXPLORER NOTES: *Timeline of bug evolution*

WORMS — CRUSTACEANS — MYRIAPODS — ARACHNIDS — INSECTS

Time (approx): 520 MYA — 500 MYA — 450 MYA — 430 MYA — 415 MYA

That's classified!

To get to grips with all this diversity, scientists use a careful system of classification that helps them know exactly what's what, or at least what goes where. They put the vast majority of the animals that we call bugs into a group of hard-shelled creatures called 'arthropods'.

Arthropods are recognisable by their many jointed limbs as well as the hard exoskeletons that encase their segmented bodies. But even though all the arthropod species can be classed under this one label, the diversity that exploded in the Cambrian seas continued, and the numbers of different arthropod species that exist today go into the millions. Of all the different animal species currently living on planet Earth, an unbelievable 85 per cent are arthropods. Insects such as ants, arachnids such as spiders, myriapods such as centipedes and crustaceans such as woodlice are all arthropods, just as much as their underwater Cambrian ancestors.

The specifics

Not only are the arthropods the largest group of bugs alive today, they are the largest group of animals alive today, full stop. To make sense of all this difference, scientists divide larger groups, like the arthropods, into smaller subgroups. The Apocrita are a subgroup which includes ants, bees and wasps. But not all ants, bees and wasps are the same – so scientists have to divide these subgroups further still, into different species. The European honeybee has the species name *Apis mellifera* – *Apis* tells us that it belongs to the subgroup of 'hive bees', while *mellifera* (Greek for 'honey-bringer') tells us precisely what species this specimen might . . . bee!

'Turn the page to discover more about different types of arthropod!'

WHAT IS A BUG?

How do you identify a bug?

What's the first thing you notice when you look closely at a bug? Perhaps their unusual eyes, or maybe their brittle bodies? Perhaps their translucent wings or their spindly legs? Most bugs are classed as 'arthropods'. Scientists have discovered more than 1.2 million different arthropod species, each with its own specific characteristics. But they do have some features in common – here are some notes to show you exactly what makes a bug, a bug . . .

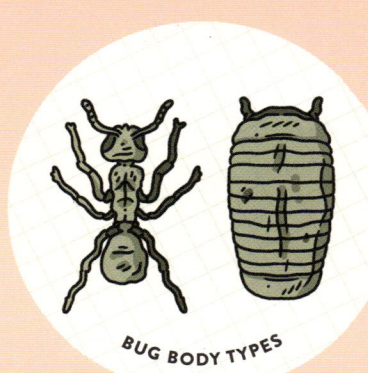

BUG BODY TYPES

What shapes are bugs' bodies?

Arthropods do not have bones structuring their bodies. Whether ants or wasps, bees or beetles, spiders or flies, their soft insides are protected by their hard, smooth 'exoskeletons' – brittle, shell-like coverings encasing their different body segments. If you look closely, you can see how these segments fit together – insects' heads are at the front of their bodies, with their mouthparts, feelers and antennae. In the middle is their 'thorax', to which the legs and wings are attached. At the back, the large bulbous blob is the 'abdomen', where internal organs are stored.

MOTH

WOODLOUSE

MILLIPEDE

WHAT IS A BUG?

How many legs does a bug have?

Insects have six segmented legs protruding from their thorax in the middle. Spiders, scorpions and other arachnids have eight legs however, sprouting out from directly behind their heads. Millipedes play a different game entirely, with hundreds of pairs of legs running along the length of their long thoraxes, helping them clamber cautiously over rocks and plants. Smaller wrigglers like house centipedes can have up to fifteen pairs of legs, which riffle together as they escape under the floorboards out of sight.

BUG LEG LAYOUTS

FLY

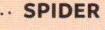

SPIDER

HUMAN EYE VIEW

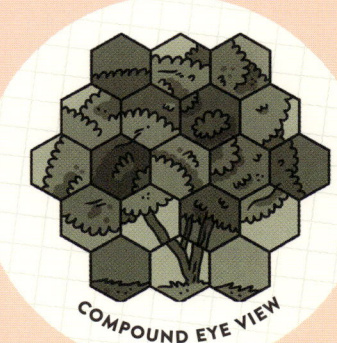
COMPOUND EYE VIEW

How do bugs see?

Some arthropods have eyes that protrude from their heads on stalks, others have eyes which take up their whole head entirely. Some bugs' eyes are so complex they can actually see in the dark. Many spiders have eight eyes, although some still have terrible vision! Most arthropods have 'compound eyes' – they see the world around them as a mosaic of hexagonal panels, which flicker when anything moves. It's a way of seeing that's so sensitive, a hexagon only needs to glimmer once before a fly gets suspicious and buzzes away.

WEEVIL

2. BUG BEGINNINGS

EAGLE-EYED LIBRARY No. 01

SCOYENIA

'Four hundred and fifty million years ago, land on Earth was barren, dusty and dry. Hot winds blew across the empty spaces. No plants grew, no animals roamed the sandy terrain. In the seas however, new forms of bug life were exploding into existence at every turn. One aquatic species escaped this frenzy and began to explore a little bit further – somewhere on a rocky shore, something slithered on to the dry land, and made a journey that changed bug life forever…'

Exploring new territory

Who was this first explorer? Some tiny burrows unearthed in North America are the oldest evidence ever found of life on land. Scientists think they were made by an ancient millipede-like myriapod, to hide from predators. Species of worm or arachnid may have moved on to the land this early too. It is still unclear which species arrived first, but this move from water to land started a brand-new chapter in the bugs' story.

A new life on dry land could not have been easy – breathing air instead of water, surviving the desert heat instead of the cool waves, even walking on dry land instead of swimming through the sea were all challenges these early explorers had to face. But life evolves and adapts to new conditions – species lost the gills for breathing underwater and began to take in oxygen from the air. Their exoskeletons protected them against the dry heat. They developed feet that helped them scrabble around. Free from predators trying to eat them or competitors trying to steal their food, the empty prehistoric landscape offered one further advantage to these early land-loving bugs – a secure place not only for individual creatures, but for their eggs as well, safely protecting the next generation.

Bug feet for walking on land

Introducing insects...

The myriapods that came on to the land may be the ancestors of the most successful group of animals ever to exist on Earth – insects. But what was the first insect? A species named *Rhyniognatha*, living 412 million years ago, is the oldest insect yet discovered, with six legs and an insect's mouthparts. In the Carboniferous period 60 million years later, a new evolutionary explosion saw insect life bloom, an evolutionary step that can be traced back to that mysterious animal that crawled out of the sea so long ago.

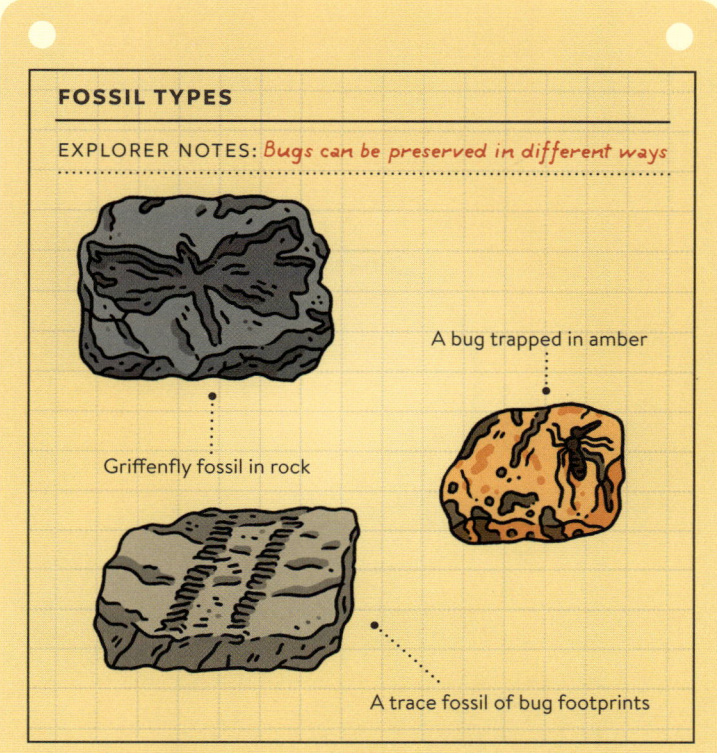

FOSSIL TYPES

EXPLORER NOTES: *Bugs can be preserved in different ways*

Griffenfly fossil in rock

A bug trapped in amber

A trace fossil of bug footprints

Rhyniognatha may have even had wings

Traces of bug life

Exploring a bed of ancient rocks in Rhynie, Scotland, scientists began to uncover fossil after fossil of ancient arachnid, centipede and insect species. Fossils are relics of the past – they are formed when the body of a living thing wastes away, and grit and soil collect in the space it leaves behind. Over time, the dirt solidifies into the exact shape of the specimen's body. Insects, dinosaurs, even plants may all turn into fossils.

An animal's environment may become fossilised too – a millipede footprint or a myriapod burrow may become a 'trace fossil', evidence of the creature's life without a fossil of the creature itself. Amber fossils form when organisms become stuck in sticky tree resin. Unable to move, they eventually die, but over centuries the sap solidifies into amber with the creature still inside, the body preserved in perfect detail.

'Turn the page to discover more about eight-legged arachnids!'

BUG BEGINNINGS

What are arachnids?

Some of the first bugs to crawl on to land were arachnids, identifiable by their eight long legs. Over time, arachnids evolved in various ways, with different adaptations that helped them hide from predators or catch prey. Some trapped prey in their sticky webs, others hid from predators under the ground. Here are some field notes which take a closer look at the lives of the arachnids . . .

HARVESTMEN : SPECIES – *EOPHALANGIUM*

EXPLORER NOTES: *10mm-long with hooked legs and foul-smelling spray*

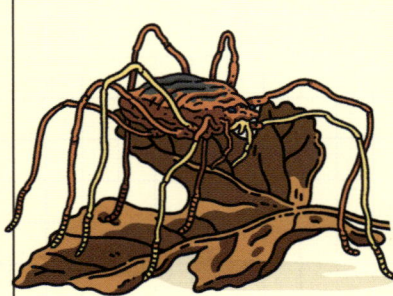

The long legs of a harvestman make it look a lot like a spider, but their bodies are differently shaped, and they cannot produce silk. They flick through the fields at harvest time, scavenging for prey through piles of autumn leaves. If a predator attacks, harvestmen fight back by squirting out a foul-smelling stinky spray directly from their abdomen.

TIMELINE DATE *410 million years ago*

TRIGONOTARBIDS : SPECIES – *PALAEOTARBUS*

EXPLORER NOTES: *1.35mm-long, spider-like arachnid predator*

Palaeotarbus was a trigonotarbid, some of the earliest arachnids to evolve. Although they looked like spiders, they couldn't spin webs, and crawled over the ground to hunt down their prey of early flightless insects. Mass extinctions 290 million years ago saw the end of many groups of animals – like so many others, the trigonotarbids were swept away, never to exist again.

TIMELINE DATE *422 million years ago*

MITES AND TICKS : SPECIES – *PROTOCARUS*

EXPLORER NOTES: *Less than 0.5mm-long, small size lets it hitch rides on other animals unnoticed*

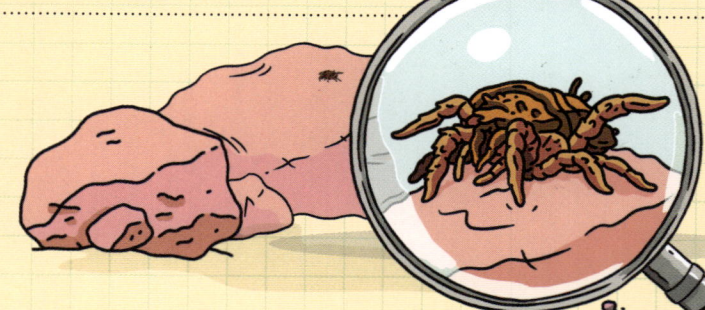

Hidden safely underground, tiny arachnids like *Protocarus* are mites that feed on fungi under the soil. Ticks are mites too – they live above ground, and wait patiently on leaves in the countryside, before dropping on to passing animals to suck their blood. Some mites are helpful to humans, with cheesemakers letting tiny cheese-mites feed on their ripening cheese, to get just the right tang for their dairy produce.

TIMELINE DATE *410 million years ago*

BUG BEGINNINGS

SCORPIONS | SPECIES – *PULMONOSCORPIUS*

EXPLORER NOTES: 70cm-long, fierce predator

As the stars came out, this huge scorpion was on the prowl. Almost a metre in length, *Pulmonoscorpius* was a nocturnal predator that chased down prey with its giant claws, paralysing its victims with a whip of its venom-tipped tail before munching them up. It hid away in the shadows, although if caught by the light of the moon its exoskeleton would glow a milky blue, a mysterious characteristic of all scorpions today.

TIMELINE DATE: 335 million years ago

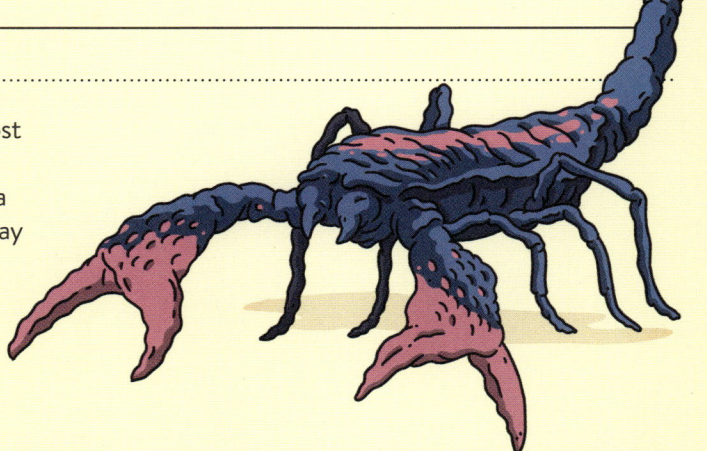

WHIP SPIDER | SPECIES – *GRAEOPHONUS*

EXPLORER NOTES: 2cm-long, sideways shuffler with vicious pincers

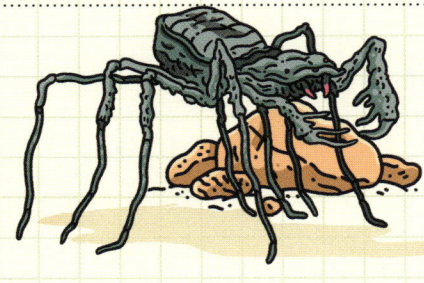

Winding its long wiry legs outwards as it hunts down its prey, whip spiders are sly hunters that scrabble along sideways as they chase down their victims. They are not at all afraid of humans, slipping into people's houses at night, where they hide away in dark cracks before scuttling out to hunt smaller species with their enormous fanged pincers.

TIMELINE DATE: 314 million years ago

SPIDERS | SPECIES – *ROSAMYGALE*

EXPLORER NOTES: 6mm-long, hides in funnel-shaped web to trap prey

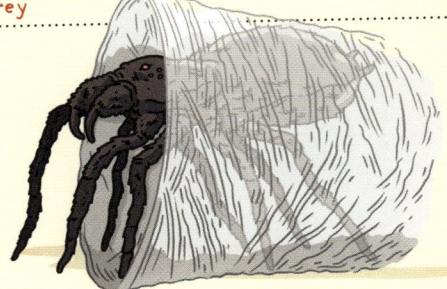

The crooked spirals of a silken web are a sure sign of a spider. Webs help spiders trap prey, but spiders can also use silk to glide through the air, with juveniles of some species floating on lines of silk to find new habitats. Funnel-web spiders like *Rosamygale* hide inside their silken lairs – adults weave strands of silk together to make their own fuzzy funnels, then sit inside their woven burrows, silently waiting, before shooting out to grab prey with their sharp fangs.

TIMELINE DATE: 245 million years ago

3. GIANT BUGS

MEGANEURA AND ARCHIMYLACRIS

'The Carboniferous period saw plant life flourish all over planet Earth. The dry dusty days of the past were gone, and in this cooler, more humid atmosphere great forests grew, and thick jungles of ferns and trees spread in green masses all over the land. In among these plants, bug life flourished with species evolving into new and massive forms, growing to sizes never seen before or since. All around, life throbbed with the buzz of insects thriving in the new emerald-green environment.'

EAGLE-EYED LIBRARY No. 04

Forests full of bugs

Zooming over a bushy horsetail plant, or hiding beneath a fern's delicate leaves, the Carboniferous forest was brimming with bug life. The atmosphere was rich with oxygen, which plants produce as they get energy from the sun. With more oxygen in the air, and more vegetation to eat, bugs grew to enormous sizes – the giant bugs of the Carboniferous were almost twice as big as the largest bugs today. Bugs' bodies contain 'spiracles' – tubes that deliver oxygen to their cells. The extra oxygen in the atmosphere could be absorbed more deeply into their bodies, helping species grow to giant proportions.

Bug breathing tubes

These massive bugs dominated the air, zipping between trees and buzzing beneath branches. Griffenflies were humongous relatives of dragonflies, with species like *Meganeura* measuring 70cm from wingtip to wingtip. They swooped between plants to catch prey, hunting other insects or grabbing amphibians hiding near brackish waters. On the ground, the forest trails were bustling with dusky cockroaches, which made up 60 per cent of insect species at that time. They hissed through the undergrowth, their spindly antennae winding back and forth.

Vanishing giants

Cockroaches and dragonflies still exist today, but why did the gigantic bugs disappear? Oxygen levels in the atmosphere began to fall, which may have led to many of the giant species like *Meganeura* dying out. In this altered environment, smaller species began to dominate – neopterans were new kinds of insects, better able to withstand the changed conditions. Not only did they take over from the Carboniferous giants, they continue to be the most widespread type of insects existing today. Long after the Carboniferous, in the Jurassic period, other types of flying animal were evolving too – birds had begun to appear, which challenged the insects in the skies. For a hungry *Archaeopteryx*, perhaps the first bird to fly, a gigantic flying insect was hard to miss, but easy to gobble up.

Giant millipede Arthropleura *and flying insect* Mazothairos

Gigantic creatures

Other kinds of bugs in the Carboniferous jungle grew to enormous proportions too. *Arthropleura* was a millipede, which wound its incredibly long two-metre body over tree roots and through fallen leaves, on the search for fungus and plants to eat. Scientists can even trace its journeys through the undergrowth today by studying the trace fossils its many footprints left behind. Other giant insects whizzed through the air – *Mazothairos* was a massive wide-winged flier, shooting around beneath the Carboniferous sun with its half-metre wingspan. It touched down on plants and pierced into plant stems with its tubular mouthparts, sucking out the gooey sap inside.

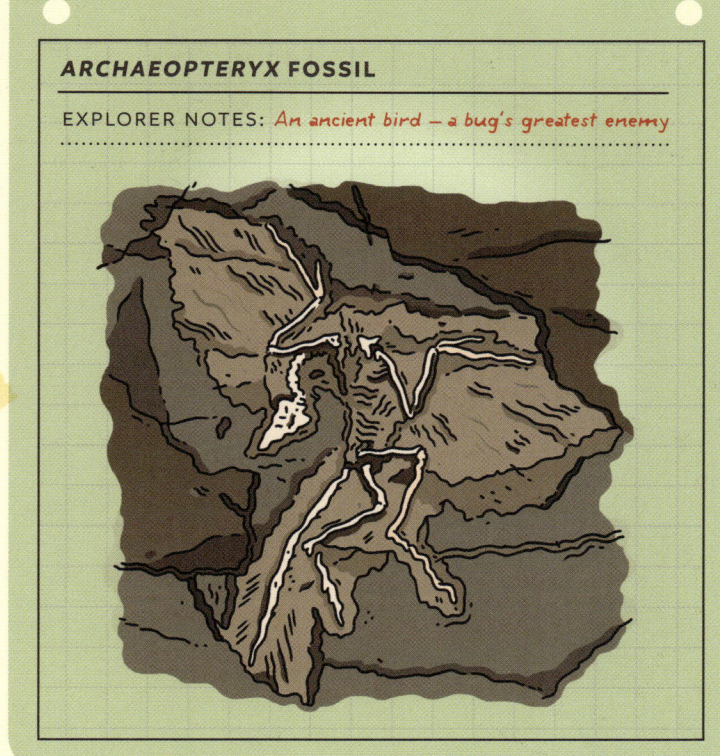

ARCHAEOPTERYX FOSSIL

EXPLORER NOTES: *An ancient bird – a bug's greatest enemy*

'Turn the page to discover how flying bugs developed!'

GIANT BUGS

Do all bugs have wings?

When explorers try to figure out how ancient species evolved, they need a place to start. Flightless silverfish, firebrats and jumping bristletails today resemble the earliest wingless insects. Maybe after simply falling from Carboniferous trees, 'parachuting' to the ground to find food or breed, similar ancient insects began to evolve with wings, taking control of a leap into the unknown.

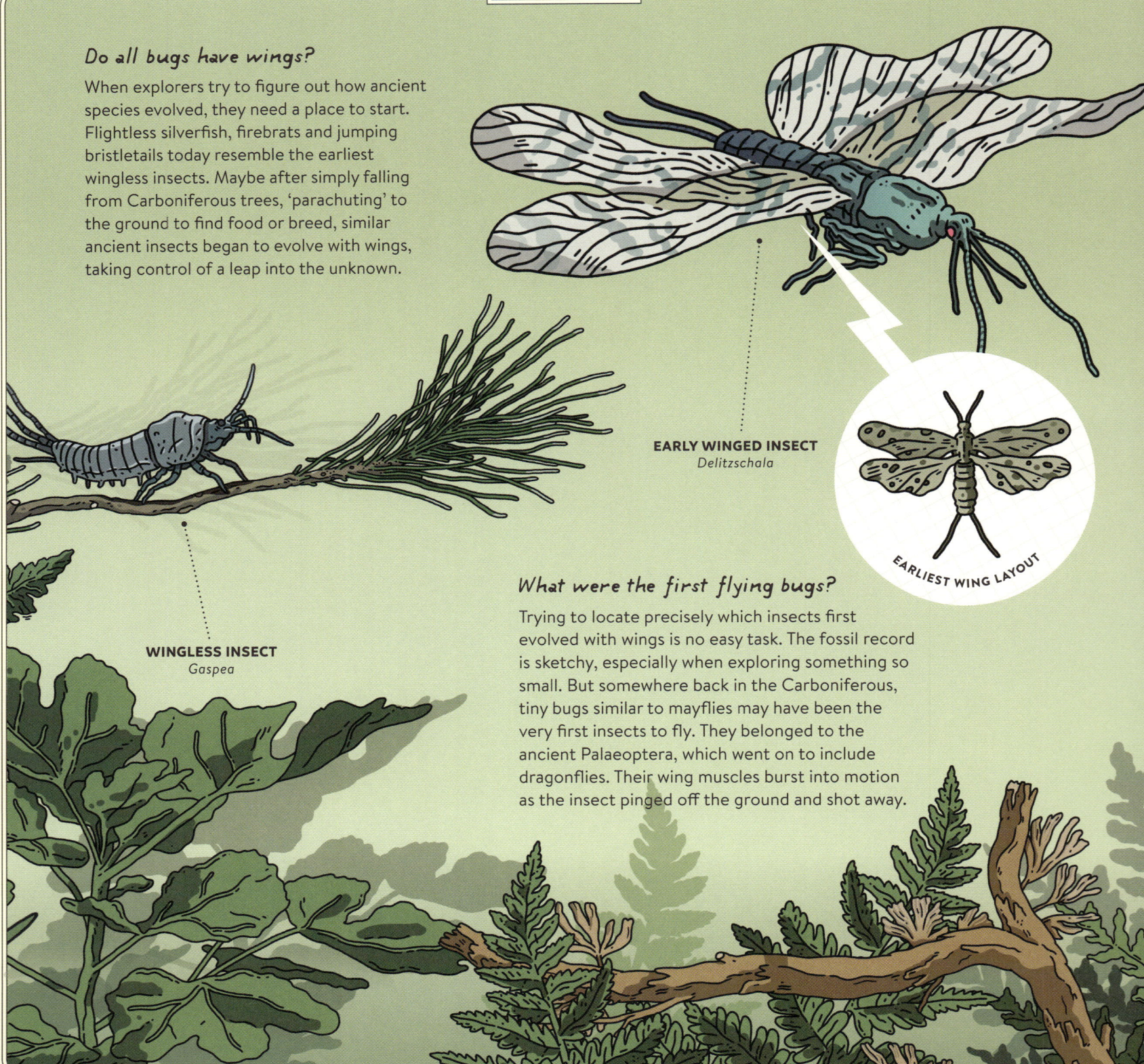

EARLY WINGED INSECT
Delitzschala

WINGLESS INSECT
Gaspea

EARLIEST WING LAYOUT

What were the first flying bugs?

Trying to locate precisely which insects first evolved with wings is no easy task. The fossil record is sketchy, especially when exploring something so small. But somewhere back in the Carboniferous, tiny bugs similar to mayflies may have been the very first insects to fly. They belonged to the ancient Palaeoptera, which went on to include dragonflies. Their wing muscles burst into motion as the insect pinged off the ground and shot away.

GIANT BUGS

How did bugs find better ways to fly?

As insects continued to evolve, their methods of flying evolved too – the neopteran insects were sophisticated fliers that overtook the palaeopterans, which were mostly wiped out in a mass extinction. For neopteran insects, flight was a tricky operation – they squeezed their wing muscles at rapid speeds, with neopteran bumblebees beating their wings 250 times per second, creating a buzzing sound. Palaeopterans, such as long blue damselflies with their stretched-out horizontal wings, only managed to beat their wings 15 times per second, lagging way behind as the neopterans zoomed off into the undergrowth.

MOSQUITO (FLY)
Burmaculex

MOTH (NEOPTERAN)
Archaeolepis

What are the best bug fliers?

The bodies of the Diptera, or 'true flies', evolved in a way that enabled them to steer through the air with precision, weaving around obstacles, ducking away from predators. If you examine them closely, you can see exactly how they manage it – all winged insects have two pairs of wings, but on the Diptera, one pair became much smaller as they evolved. The Diptera use these 'halteres' as compact steering rudders to help them control their flight in the most precise way.

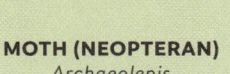

4. BUG LIFE

DRAGONFLY

'Metamorphosis. A mysterious word, with a mysterious meaning, but an essential part of growing up for many different bug species. How can a pale and squidgy maggot be the same creature as a dark and gnarly fly? Why does its body change from one form into another? How does this transformation happen? How do young bugs survive without the wings and stingers that adults need for protection? And what on earth is a pupa?'

Metamorphosis

'Metamorphosis' is the name of the process where a creature's body changes entirely from one form to another as it grows. It happens throughout the insect world, where bugs' bodies transform in dramatic ways between infancy and adulthood.

Dragonflies hatch out as 'nymphs', stubby swimmers that scoot about underwater hunting for food. As they develop into adults, their bodies grow bigger and more colourful, sprouting wings for chasing prey in the air. But infant scorpionflies hatch out as 'larvae' instead – soft, tiny maggots – before they 'metamorphose' into wiry adults with spiky tails, changing shape completely. Similarly, infant butterflies start life as bulging caterpillars. As a caterpillar grows, it changes into a 'pupa', wrapping itself in silk to form a 'chrysalis'. After several weeks, the caterpillar emerges from its chrysalis transformed. It dries its newly developed wings in the air, before fluttering away as a butterfly.

But why do bugs metamorphose in the first place? Their different bodies mean adults and infants have different needs and can live side by side without competing for food or shelter. It's an evolutionary adaptation that has helped bugs survive for millions of years.

Inside a chrysalis

Hide and seek

A compact body might protect your internal organs, but other animals might see a plump caterpillar as a tasty snack. To trick predators into thinking they're not there, some caterpillars have evolved to look like plants. Other caterpillars eat poisonous shrubs, storing the toxic juices in their spines to poison their enemies. Some species are even disguised as bird poo to really put predators off. Other creatures have evolved with a particularly grisly way of making sure their newborns have something to eat: venomous wasps sting other animals into paralysis, then lay their eggs on top of – or even inside – their victims' paralysed bodies. When the wasp larvae hatch, the animal can only lie helpless as the newborns start to feed.

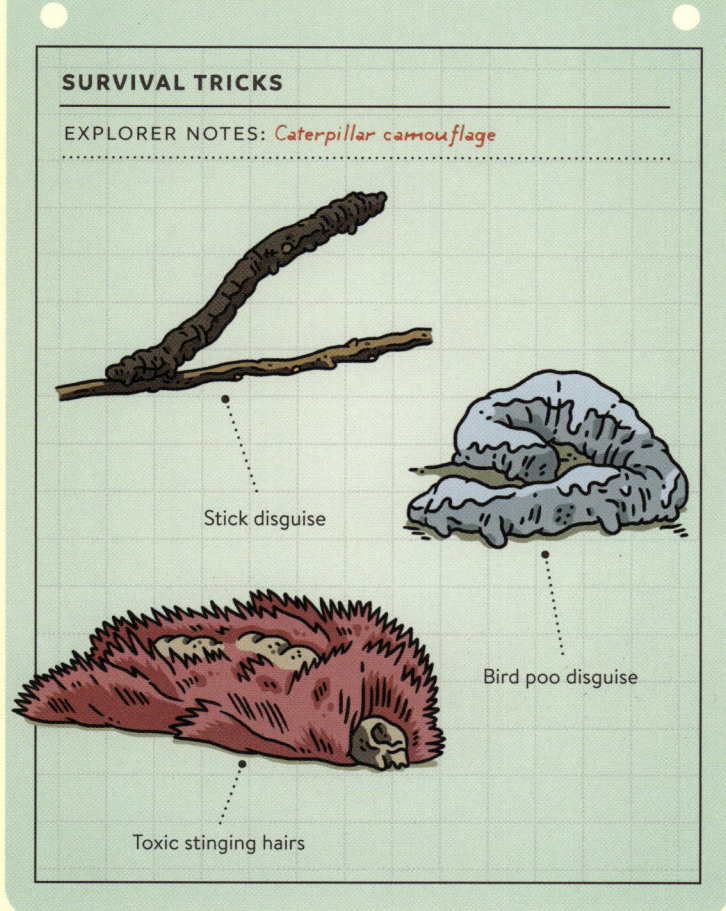

SURVIVAL TRICKS

EXPLORER NOTES: *Caterpillar camouflage*

- Stick disguise
- Bird poo disguise
- Toxic stinging hairs

Female praying mantis eating its mate

The art of attraction

Before laying their eggs, adults have to find a mate. Different species have evolved different ways of getting noticed – cicadas emit a deafening buzz to attract attention; fireflies' bodies blink in the dark with chemically produced lights; butterflies simply open their colourful patterned wings to demonstrate their magnificence to potential mates.

Other species are more creative. Some spiders and scorpionflies like to bring along a gift of a dead insect, for potential partners to suck on. Some male scorpionflies even bring the used gift to a new female partner, hoping their luck hasn't run out. When searching for a mate, male praying mantises tend to avoid any females that might look a little peckish – female mantises mate with males, but may well decide to eat them up afterwards too.

'Turn the page to discover what clever strategies bugs use to survive!'

BUG LIFE

What special strategies do bugs use to stay alive?

Different bug species have evolved in various ways that help them survive in their environments. Some bugs have camouflage to avoid predators; others build defences to protect themselves as a colony. Some sing special songs to attract mates; some have sneaky disguises to avoid attention entirely. All the different species of bugs have evolved with their own specific survival strategies, as my notes will reveal…

DISGUISES | BUTTERFLIES, MOTHS AND LACEWINGS

EXPLORER NOTES: *Uses threatening eye spots to scare off attackers*

Some butterflies, moths and lacewings are mimics that scare off predators by pretending to be something they're not. The intricate patterns on their wings look just like the eyes of bigger, more dangerous animals, terrifying enemies away. They use their long proboscises to tap into plant stems and suck out the juices inside, flashing their eye spots if danger creeps up behind them.

SPECIES NAME *Kaligramma*
TIMELINE DATE *165 million years ago*

HOME SECURITY | WEB-SPINNERS

EXPLORER NOTES: *Drapes its entire territory with its own web*

These web-spinning insects crawl between cracks and crevices in the earth, leaving a silken trail behind them, draping their dark underground territory entirely with silvery webs. Large populations live together in these pale habitats, known as 'galleries'. They expand these further as the group forages for food, protected by the ghostly grey tunnels they create under the earth.

SPECIES NAME *Palaeomesorthopteron*
TIMELINE DATE *245 million years ago*

HIDING UNDERGROUND | MOLE CRICKETS

EXPLORER NOTES: *Sings underground to attract mating partners*

Mole crickets stay out of sight underground, safely hidden from predators, munching on roots in the soil. But sometimes individuals want to be noticed – males dig out spaces in the earth where sound can resonate, and rub their legs together to 'sing' to potential mating partners above. Intrigued females scurry around on the surface, trying to figure out where the seductive sound is coming from.

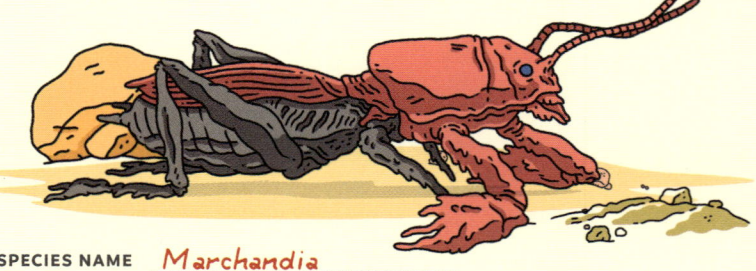

SPECIES NAME *Marchandia*
TIMELINE DATE *105 million years ago*

| BUG LIFE |

CAMOUFLAGE : STICK AND LEAF INSECTS

EXPLORER NOTES: *Camouflaged as plants to fool predators*

The bodies of stick insects have evolved in a way that imitates the twigs and branches in their environment. Species like ancient *Eophyllium* have bodies shaped like little leaves. If a stick insect stands stock still, predators won't even know it's there and pass by to find other prey instead, as the camouflaged stick insect disappears into the surrounding foliage.

SPECIES NAME: *Eophyllium*
TIMELINE DATE: *45 million years ago*

VENOMOUS STINGS : WASPS

EXPLORER NOTES: *Egg-laying tool turned into vicious stinger*

Ants, bees and wasps lay their eggs through tube-like 'ovipositors' protruding from the end of their bodies. Their ancestors used them to pierce into plants for storing their young inside. On modern wasps, the ovipositors have evolved into sharp stingers, which can pierce into flesh and inject a painful shot of venom to combat attackers or paralyse prey. Some wasps then lay their eggs inside the victim, while others use their stings just as a weapon.

SPECIES NAME: *Palaeovespa*
TIMELINE DATE: *44 million years ago*

IRRITATING HAIRS : TARANTULAS

EXPLORER NOTES: *Large, venomous carnivore*

Big, hairy and with venomous fangs, a tarantula is not the sort of creature you would like to cross paths with in the jungle. They use their spiked fangs to trap insects, lizards or frogs, injecting prey with poison before eating them up. They might not have the stomach for human beings, but the hairs they shed from their abdomens are powerful irritants and can even turn attackers blind.

SPECIES NAME: *Clostes*
TIMELINE DATE: *35 million years ago*

5. BUG COMMUNITIES

MASTOTERMES

'Some bugs defend themselves with their poisonous stingers; other bugs have sharp fangs to help them catch their food. But some species have evolved with a completely different secret to their survival — they look after each other. Many bug species live together in huge societies, where various members of the community perform particular roles essential to the group's survival. For some insects, society is such an essential part of their lives, individuals couldn't survive if stranded on their own.'

Termites

Out on the African savannah a craggy tower stands alone on the plain, a gigantic construction, as tall as the nearby trees, red and brown like the dry earth all around. Crawling in and out of this huge mound are the tiny creatures that built it – termites. The mound can be nine metres tall, forming a gigantic nest where the termites live together in their thousands or even millions. In this bustling termite society, different groups carry out their own tasks that are essential to the whole community's survival. Worker termites find food and look after the young. Soldiers protect the colony from danger.

Soldier, queen and worker termites

Insects were the first animals to live together in societies, with species discovering the benefits of working together long ago. Cockroaches are ancient insects which look after their young when they hatch, protecting their own infants even if only for short amounts of time. Termites evolved from ancient cockroach species around 140 million years ago in the Cretaceous period and began not only to look after their young, but each other as well, living side-by-side in colonies. It's a way of life that has been so successful, termites continue to survive together in their mounds today.

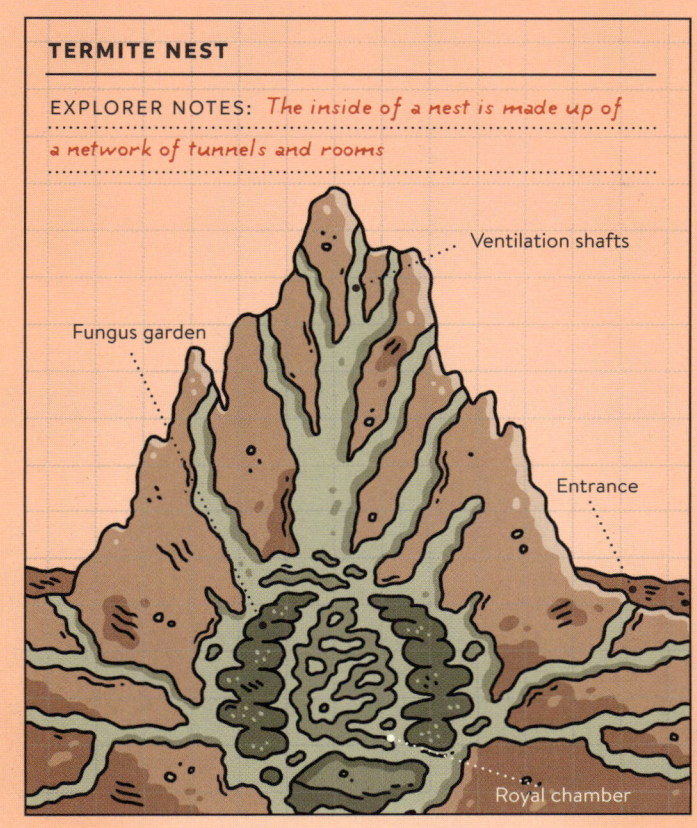

TERMITE NEST

EXPLORER NOTES: *The inside of a nest is made up of a network of tunnels and rooms*

- Ventilation shafts
- Fungus garden
- Entrance
- Royal chamber

Social living

Many wasps, ants and bees build nests where they live together in societies too. Honey ants have developed a special way of storing food – workers' bodies are filled up with nectar, which they cough up for other ants to feed on when supplies are scarce. Paper wasps chew up wood or plants to build their nests, which they hang from trees or inside the roof of a house. Infant wasp larvae need stable temperatures, which the nest can provide, as well as serving as a strong defence against predators. When the nest is disturbed however, wasps use their venomous sting to attack the predators. The nest and the stingers all serve a royal purpose: to defend the queen and her brood of infant wasps.

Paper wasp nest

Life inside the colony

A termite nest is made of many tunnels and spaces, interconnecting like rooms in a medieval castle. The infants are kept in a special chamber, where they are fed by worker termites. The food is prepared inside the mound – worker termites mix plants with a special fungus, making meals for the infants and soldiers. The soldiers defend the nest using a chemical they spray from their heads. Deep inside the nest, in their own personal quarters, are the kings and queens. Their job is to reproduce, to fill up the colony with new termites and keep the community alive. Each queen produces young at a crazy rate – every few seconds a new egg is laid. When the egg hatches, a new termite will be born, ready to grow into its role as a worker or a soldier, or maybe even to grow up and move off to new territory to start a new colony of its own.

'Turn the page to discover the different ways bugs communicate!'

BUG COMMUNITIES

How do bugs communicate with movement?

When honeybees discover a new source of food or a great spot to build a new nest, they have to tell the other bees about it back in the beehive. They communicate the news in a unique way – using the power of dance. They waggle their bodies to show the direction to go and bustle in loops to show the distance that must be travelled, wiggling their fuzzy bums before each new instruction. The audience of other bees carefully watch, ready to get busy.

BEE DANCE ROUTINE

HONEY BEE
Apis

CICADA
Burmacicada

How do bugs communicate through sound?

Deep in the shady woods, a hissing, scratching noise vibrates at maximum volume through the trees. The buzz comes from insects called cicadas which are hidden out of sight, but make a sound so painfully loud their presence is unmistakable. Individuals switch off their own hearing organs as they 'sing' to avoid the horror of such a loud racket. The noise lets other cicadas know they're there, each individual looking for another cicada to mate with.

BUG COMMUNITIES

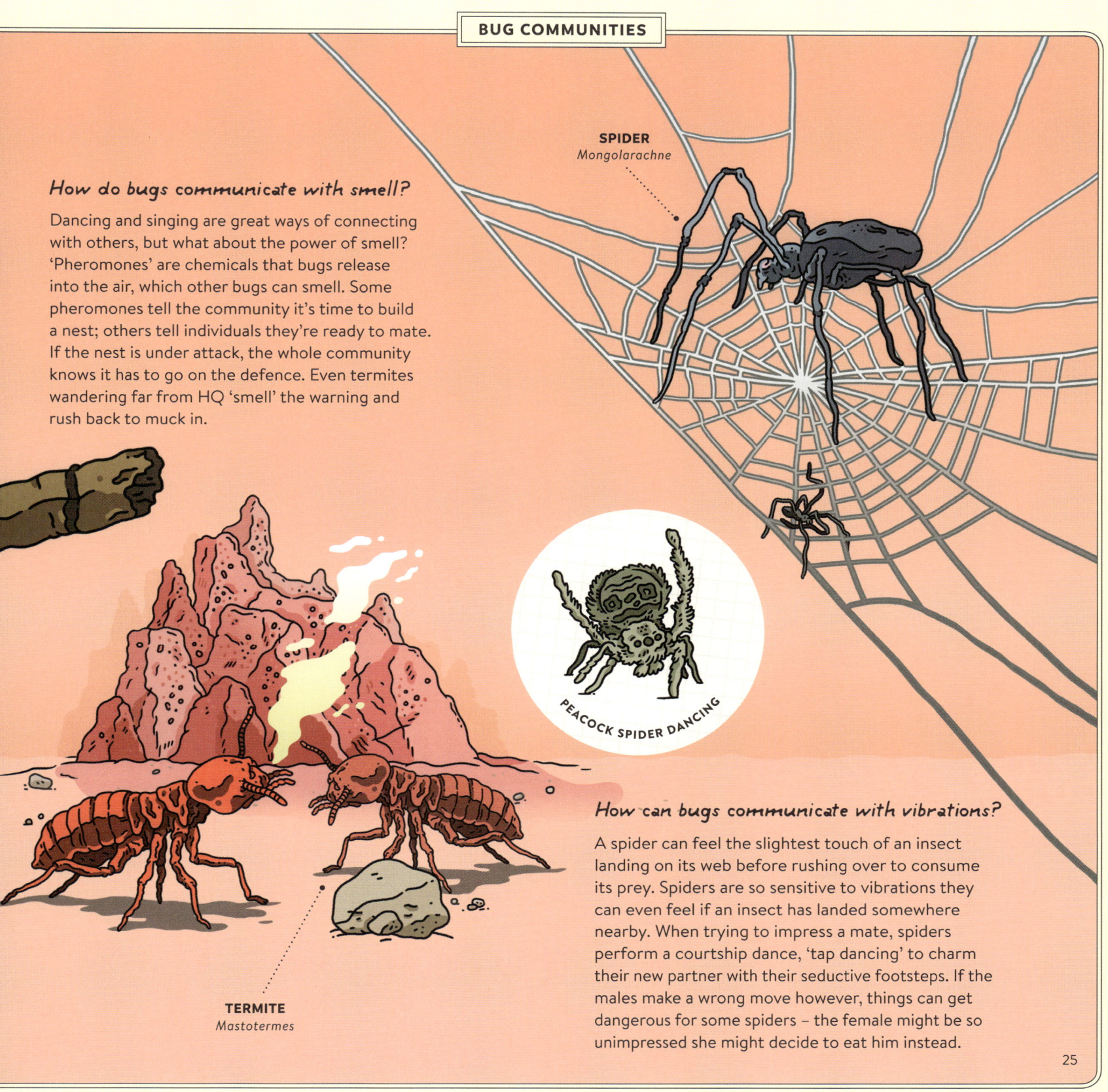

How do bugs communicate with smell?

Dancing and singing are great ways of connecting with others, but what about the power of smell? 'Pheromones' are chemicals that bugs release into the air, which other bugs can smell. Some pheromones tell the community it's time to build a nest; others tell individuals they're ready to mate. If the nest is under attack, the whole community knows it has to go on the defence. Even termites wandering far from HQ 'smell' the warning and rush back to muck in.

SPIDER
Mongolarachne

PEACOCK SPIDER DANCING

TERMITE
Mastotermes

How can bugs communicate with vibrations?

A spider can feel the slightest touch of an insect landing on its web before rushing over to consume its prey. Spiders are so sensitive to vibrations they can even feel if an insect has landed somewhere nearby. When trying to impress a mate, spiders perform a courtship dance, 'tap dancing' to charm their new partner with their seductive footsteps. If the males make a wrong move however, things can get dangerous for some spiders – the female might be so unimpressed she might decide to eat him instead.

6. BUGS AND HUMANS

XENOPSYLLA

'Humans have always lived in a close relationship with bugs. Early civilisations worshipped bugs and saw how bugs' lives reflected the way the world worked. Bugs were part of their culture and were used as symbols of life and death. They discovered how to farm bugs and the miraculous powers of the food bugs produce. But sometimes bugs and humans got too close, with deadly consequences. Here are some notes on the connections between human society and bug life.'

The Black Death

In the fourteenth century, all over Europe, people were falling victim to a deadly disease. Sufferers felt faint as huge blobs began to grow out of their necks, or as their skin turned grey, before their feet fell off. The disease was named the 'Black Death' and threatened everyone on the continent. The Black Death was a ravaging plague that was being spread by a bug – the Oriental rat flea. These insects would feed on rats and pick up a lethal bacteria named *Yersina pestis* from the rats' blood. It wasn't long before the fleas hopped on to a human and bit into their body as well, transferring the virus into the person's bloodstream. As the fleas bounced around, the virus spread from community to community.

The plague originated in China, but moved westwards as a result of humans using it as a weapon in warfare with one army deliberately infecting the other. Travelling along international routes, the plague spread rapidly into Europe, infecting rats, fleas and humans in their millions. People even gave the plague to each other through sneezing. In some regions one in three people died from the plague. The Black Death was a dark chapter in the history of human–bug relations.

Spread of the Black Death

Sacred scarabs

Bugs may have brought problems to some societies, but for other civilisations bugs were sacred. The Ancient Egyptians believed scarab beetles had a special relationship with the sun and painted the sun god Khepri with a scarab for his head. Scarabs are dung beetles which roll their balls of dung across the land, just as Khepri rolled the sun across the sky, from sunrise to sunset. The Egyptians crafted 'heart scarabs' for the dead and scarab-shaped jewellery for protection in the afterlife. Scarabs keep their eggs inside their dung balls, which provide a source of food when the infants hatch. The juvenile bugs eventually leave the dung ball, emerging from the dark into the light, just as the sun comes up every morning, out of the night into the day.

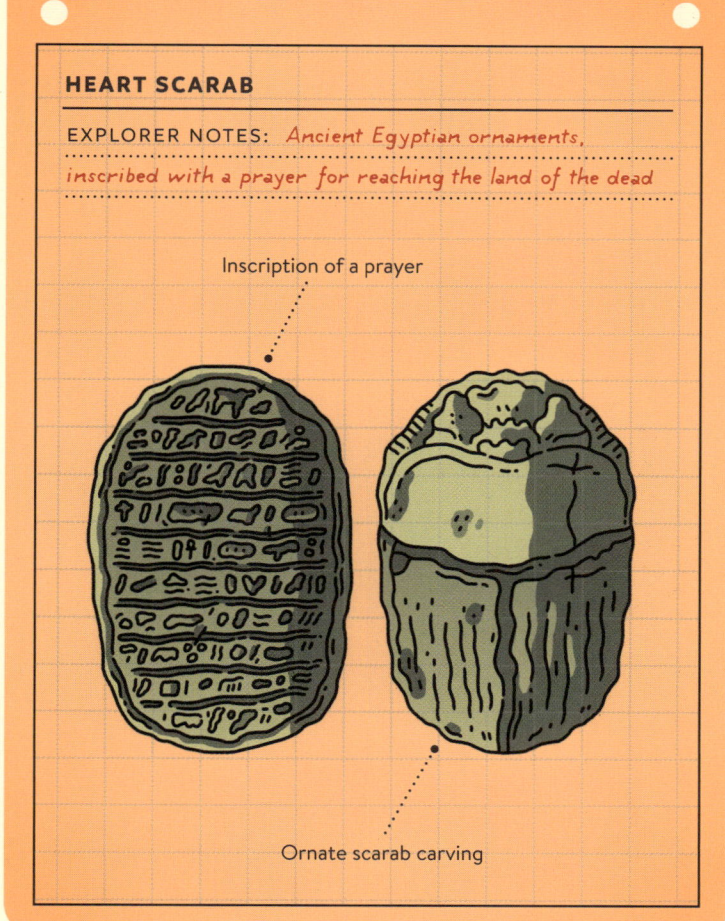

HEART SCARAB

EXPLORER NOTES: *Ancient Egyptian ornaments, inscribed with a prayer for reaching the land of the dead*

Inscription of a prayer

Ornate scarab carving

Before sugar was discovered, honey was especially popular

The ancient power of honey

The Ancient Egyptians were one of the oldest civilisations to keep bees for their honey, crafting beehives out of clay. The Egyptians loved honey's sweet taste and even used honey to preserve dead bodies. Honey stays fresh for an incredibly long time – 4,000-year-old jars of Egyptian honey are still edible today. To make honey, female bees gather nectar from flowers, then transfer it to other bees back at the hive who cough it up as honey into a honeycomb. The bees rely on their honey for food, so humans have to be careful not to take too much. Out in the wild other animals want to get their hands – or paws – on the honey too. Bears will risk a bee sting or two to break into a beehive and get a taste of one of their favourite foods.

'Turn the page to discover some of the greatest bug Explorers of all time!'

BUGS AND HUMANS

Who are the great bug Explorers?

Humans have been studying bugs for a very long time. Some Explorers discovered how to use bugs to make cloth; others believed bugs could cure the sick. Some made detailed paintings to learn the secrets of bug life; other Explorers watched how bugs change in each generation. Some Explorers discovered life on Earth could not exist without the work bugs do. I've put together some research notes on some of the most important bug Explorers and their revolutionary bug discoveries.

SUSHRUTA : Around 600 BC

EXPLORER NOTES: *Prescribed blood-sucking bugs to patients*

Bugs might even help humans recover from sickness – at least according to Sushruta, an ancient Indian doctor who used leeches to cure sick patients. Sushruta taught that illness comes from having too much blood, and the best way to drain it is by fastening a leech to the patient's body. Leeches bite into animals and suck out their blood to feed. These ideas travelled to Europe, where doctors sometimes got carried away, letting their leeches suck out so much blood their sick patients turned into dead ones!

EMPRESS LEIZU : Around 2500 BC

EXPLORER NOTES: *Unravelled the secret of silk*

In Chinese legend, Empress Leizu discovered silk when a silkworm's cocoon unravelled in her hot tea, spooling out strands of the precious fabric. China kept silk a precious guarded secret, but two travelling priests had other ideas, and smuggled silkworm eggs out of Asia inside their wooden staffs. But silkworms are killed whenever silk is made, so perhaps it would be better for the silkworm if the secret had been kept under wraps entirely.

MARIA SIBYLLA MERIAN : 1647–1717

EXPLORER NOTES: *Painted bug life in dazzling detail*

This German explorer painted detailed pictures of insects and other bugs, a passion that began as a youngster when she sketched creepy-crawlies she found at home. In South America she made careful studies of bugs' lives, painting bright images showing how insects move, eat, fight, even transform from caterpillars into butterflies. She combined science with art and made new discoveries about bug life that challenged the ideas of men who thought science was not for girls.

BUGS AND HUMANS

CHARLES DARWIN : 1809–1882

EXPLORER NOTES: *Recognised the vital importance of the 'lowly earthworm'*

This biologist was one of the first Explorers to recognise how species evolve, changing the way humans understood nature. He studied wildlife of all kinds, but there was one bug he admired especially – the earthworm. Earthworms' tunnels bring fresh air underground and keep soil healthy for plants to grow. Without plants, there would be no food to eat, animals would starve and oxygen would disappear from the air, making earthworms one of the most important animals on our planet.

THOMAS HUNT MORGAN : 1866–1945

EXPLORER NOTES: *Studied bugs to see what children inherit from their parents*

Room 613 in Columbia University, New York, went by the name of 'the Fly Room'. Inside were the fruit flies Thomas Hunt Morgan investigated, hanging rotten bananas from the ceiling for the flies to feed on. Fruit flies reproduce very quickly, making it easy to see similarities or differences between parents and their offspring. These patterns apply to all creatures, but Morgan's bugs showed scientists exactly how the process works.

MIRIAM ROTHSCHILD : 1908–2005

EXPLORER NOTES: *Figured out insect acrobatics*

This Explorer believed not only that all people should be treated equally, but all animals as well – bugs included. In her books, she described 500 different species of flea, which she analysed from her father's collection of 30,000 fleas. She tried to understand how it was that fleas can jump incredible distances and solved the riddle of why some caterpillars deliberately eat poisonous plants – they keep the poison in their spines to prick into pesky predators.

7. PLANET OF THE BUGS

APIS

'Humans and bugs connect in many different ways, often without people even noticing. A mosquito might whine around the room, but secretly be carrying a deadly disease. The food that you buy in the supermarket might come from plants that bugs helped to grow. Bugs might also provide humans with food in several ways, a secret some cultures already know about. There are many ways that bugs and humans interact, and here's some notes explaining how...'

Picking up the pollen

Out on a summer meadow, flowers grow in bright colours, filling the air with a sweet aroma, enticing bees and other bugs buzzing all around. The bees feed on the flowers' nectar and gather the flowers' pollen on to special hairs on their legs, called pollen baskets, to bring back to the hive. The bees rely on the flowers' nectar and pollen as food for the other bees in the nest. But the flowers rely on the bees too, in a very special way. The plants need their pollen to be transported, to spread out and reach other plants to help them reproduce and create the next generation. When the bees travel from flower to flower, they bring the pollen with them, helping to fertilise the new flowers' seeds – seeds from which new plants will grow.

Plants have always relied on the work that bees and other bugs do – just as other animals have always relied on plants. For human beings, the plants that grow around us are important sources of food, medicine, even the oxygen we breathe. Today however, environmental damage caused by humans threatens the lives not only of plants, but of bees and other insects too. If there are no bugs to disperse the pollen, plants, bugs and human beings face a risky future.

Pollen baskets

Deadly diseases

Sometimes, however, bugs may be extremely unhelpful too. Mosquitoes are insects that prick into other animals to feed on their blood. In some regions of the world, mosquitoes are the main cause for the spread of the deadly disease malaria. Malaria is caused by a parasite named *Plasmodium* from a group of incredibly small microorganisms called protozoans. A mosquito might pick up the *Plasmodium* parasite from the animal it feeds on, and then transfer the disease into whatever creature it lands on next – which may well be a human being. Four hundred thousand people die every year from malaria, which can start with a headache or a fever, but then blow up into a violent illness, with chills and breathing difficulties before the sufferer passes away. Travellers in malaria regions protect themselves with nets to keep the mozzies out, or anti-malaria tablets which keep the body safe.

BUG DINING

EXPLORER NOTES: *Digging into a plate of bugs*

Locust

Tarantula

Mealworm

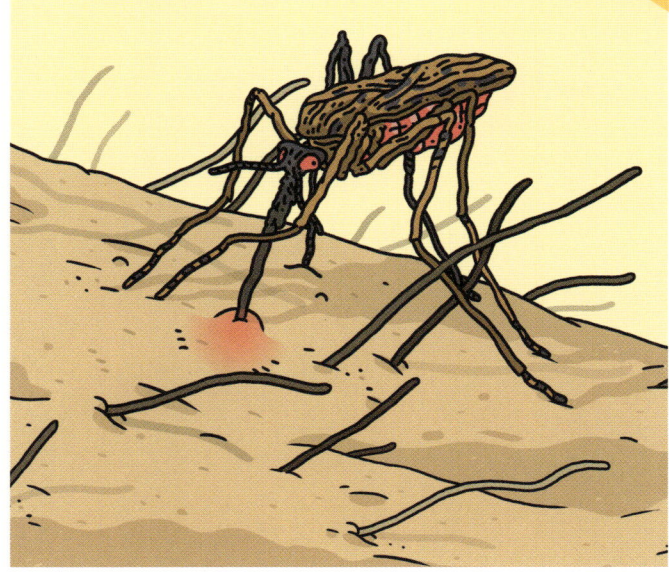

Mosquitoes suck blood with their long, piercing mouthparts

Bugs for breakfast

If a plague of insects ravages your crops and leaves you with nothing to eat, why not eat the insects instead? Bugs form part of the diet of many cultures around the world, where people enjoy eating beetles, ants, termites and even tarantulas. Other cultures don't like to think of bugs as food, although if people happily eat crustaceans like lobsters and crabs, why not eat a crustacean like a woodlouse as well? Top scientists have advised that in the future, humans will need to find new sources of food – for societies that still find eating crawly creatures creepy, maybe they can learn from those with bug-eating experience. If you're worried about the health of the planet, bite into a bug!

'Turn the page to discover how bugs may be the true rulers of Planet Earth!'

PLANET OF THE BUGS

Are bugs the oldest animals on dry land?

On an early summer night, under the silver light of a full moon, beaches across the North American coast become lined with thousands of horseshoe crabs. These bulky marine creatures come on to land to breed in safety, a habit that hasn't changed for 420 million years. Today however, it's not only predators under the sea they need to be afraid of – humans are a danger too. Fishing companies scoop up horseshoe crabs to use as bait to catch fish, and medical companies capture horseshoe crabs to experiment with their blood.

JEWEL BEETLE
Psiloptera

WEEVIL
Burmonyx

WOOD-BORING BEETLE
Notocupoides

HORSESHOE CRAB
Limulus

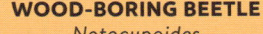

MOST ANIMAL SPECIES ARE INSECTS

Have bugs taken over the Earth?

Of all the different animal species that exist on Earth today, an astonishing 80 per cent are insects, with perhaps 30 million different species crawling around on planet Earth at this very moment. Although beetles were late developers, evolving 100 million years after the first kinds of insects emerged, they now exist in their millions, some of the most numerous on planet Earth. Mammal species, like cats or dogs or human beings, only exist in the thousands, nothing compared to our insect neighbours.

PLANET OF THE BUGS

How have bugs conquered new environments?

Locusts are plant-feeding grasshoppers and generally flightless, solitary insects. But when lots of food is discovered, their behaviour changes radically as they begin to congregate in their billions, grow wings and spread out over vast areas of land to feed. The result is a bustling storm of hungry locusts, a dense frenetic feeding swarm thousands of miles wide, terrifying farmers who fear for their crops whenever locusts appear on the horizon. The adult locusts' also pass their ravenous hunger onto their offspring too. They will consume millions of acres of vegetation to the last leaf, a feeding frenzy that will only stop when the locusts decide to move on.

FRUIT FLY
Drosophila

COCKROACH
Archimylacris

LOCUST
Electrotettix

BUGS SURVIVE IN EVERY CLIMATE

What are the toughest bugs on Earth?

Whether dropping from great heights on to hard rocks, finding a home in the subzero temperatures of the Arctic circle or surviving the intense heat of a forest fire, bugs are some of the toughest creatures around having adapted to survive in some of the most extreme environments on our planet. Reports tell of cockroaches found crawling on the rubble after a nuclear attack that obliterated all nearby human life. Fruit flies have shown their resilience too in lab conditions, being blasted with nuclear rays which would make a human being seriously sick.

AGENT EAGLE'S BUG BRAIN-TEASERS

We've explored the whole history of bugs, from ancient prehistoric arthropods to modern bugs today. Before we deliver our report to Explorer Club HQ, it's time to test our bugs knowledge. Here are some bugs quiz questions to check we've got our facts straight...

MATCH THAT BUG

Sometimes my research notes can get a bit jumbled up – see if you can match the descriptions below to the correct type of bug at the bottom of the page. Some extra names might have got mixed in as well, so be careful with your decisions!

A. Arachnid which glows blue in moonlight

B. Insects which live together in mounds of millions

C. Bug that helps the soil stay healthy

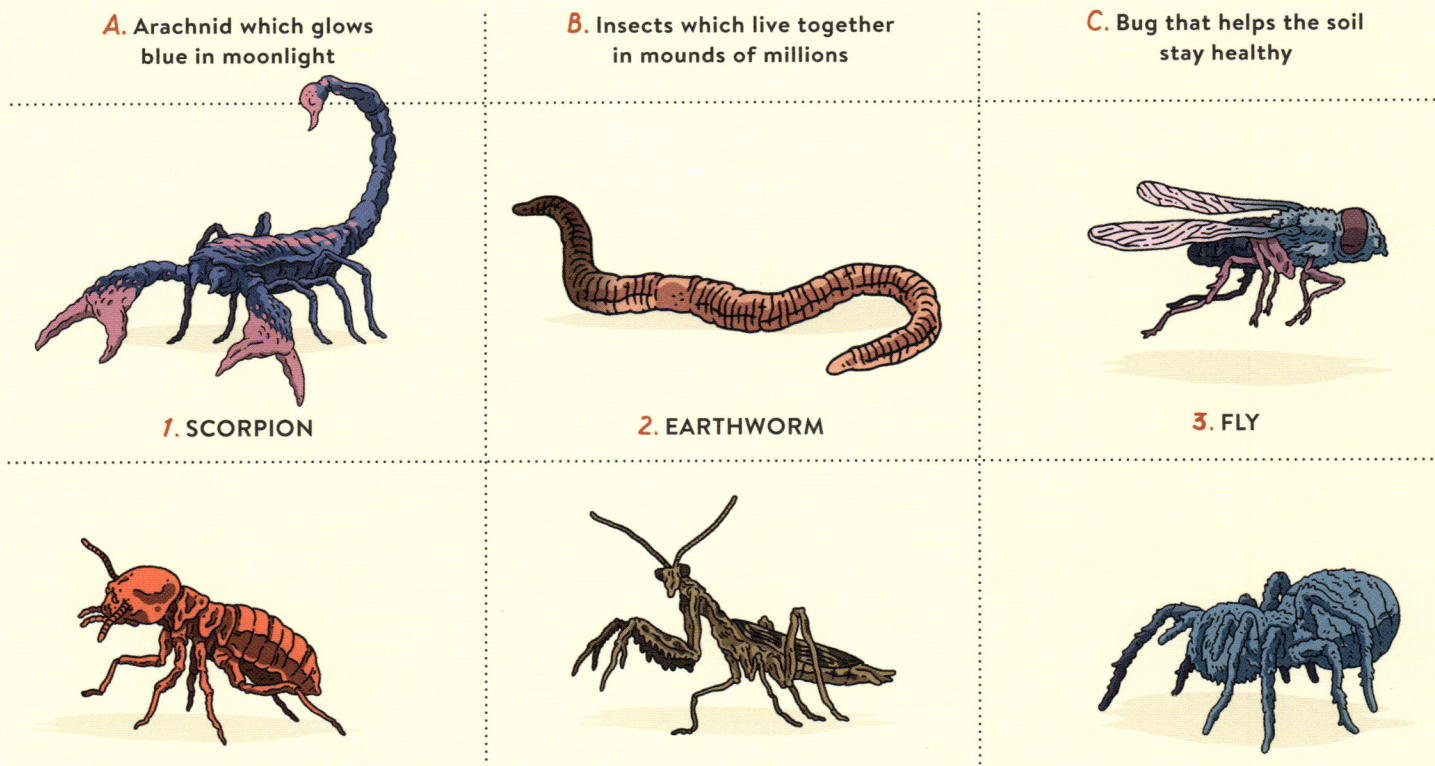

1. SCORPION   *2.* EARTHWORM   *3.* FLY

4. TERMITE   *5.* PRAYING MANTIS   *6.* SPIDER

THE BUG QUIZ
Read my report carefully to discover the answers.

1. **WHAT IS A BUG?**
Arthropods are bugs with particular characteristics. But which of these arthropod facts *isn't* true?

   a) All arthropods have hard shells called exoskeletons
   b) All arthropods have six legs
   c) All arthropod bodies have separate segments and jointed limbs

2. **BUG BEGINNINGS**
A spider's web is made out of silk. What else do spiders use silk for?

   a) They shoot it out like a lasso to trap prey
   b) They use it like a parachute to travel in the wind
   c) They wrap themselves up in silk to keep warm

3. **GIANT BUGS**
What was so special about the Carboniferous environment that helped bugs grow to gigantic sizes?

   a) There was more oxygen in the air than ever before
   b) Temperatures had never been hotter before or since
   c) It rained every day, creating the first ever monsoons

4. **BUG LIFE**
Many bugs care for their infants. How do some wasps provide food for their newborns?

   a) They collect worms for their young to eat when they hatch
   b) They paralyse prey with their sting, then lay their eggs on their victim so the offspring have a meal as soon as they hatch
   c) They cough up honey for young wasps to feed on

5. **BUG COMMUNITIES**
Some bugs live in giant bug communities. How do termites communicate with one another?

   a) By rubbing their legs together to produce a deafening buzz
   b) By dancing carefully to show other termites where to go
   c) By letting out aromatic chemicals into the air

6. **BUG AND HUMANS**
Why were scarab beetles so important to the Ancient Egyptians?

   a) They feared a pyramid would collapse whenever a scarab died
   b) Egyptians believed without scarabs, the River Nile would dry up
   c) They believed scarabs were mystically connected to the sun

7. **PLANET OF THE BUGS**
There are more arthropods on planet Earth than any other kind of animal, but what is the largest group of arthropods?

   a) Spiders
   b) Insects
   c) Toads

CLUB NOTICES

GLOSSARY

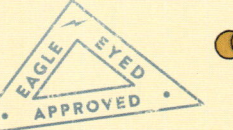

ARACHNIDS
Bugs with eight legs and usually only two main body parts. Common arachnids are spiders and scorpions.

ARTHROPODS
Animals with tough skeletons on the outside of their bodies. Most bugs are arthropods.

CAMOUFLAGE
Staying hidden by blending into the background or wearing a disguise. Bugs use camouflage to avoid predators or sneak up on prey.

COLONY
Societies where lots of bugs of the same species live together and look after each other.

CRUSTACEANS
An arthropod group. Some crustaceans, such as woodlice, live on land, but most live in water.

EVOLUTION
The process by which living organisms develop over time into new forms and become adapted to their environment.

FOSSILS
The remains of living creatures, preserved over millions of years. Fossils are used to understand ancient creatures.

INSECTS
The most common bug group. Insects have six legs and three body parts.

LARVAE
The youngest form of many bugs. Larvae are often very different to adults. Caterpillars are the larvae of butterflies and moths.

METAMORPHOSIS
A change of body shape. Many bug types metamorphose, changing their form as they develop into adults.

NECTAR
A sweet syrup produced by flowers. Many bugs drink nectar as food. Bees make nectar into honey.

PUPAE
A stage in the lifecycle of many bugs. During the pupa stage, larvae transform into adult bugs.

VENOM
Toxins used by some bugs such as wasps and scorpions to attack prey or defend against predators.

WORMS
Bugs with long, thin bodies. Some worms have segments, while others are smooth.

THE TEAM

NICK FORSHAW
Nick is a writer based in Berlin. He holds a BA and MA in film and literary studies. He hopes his readers love learning about the world and all the things in it just as much as he does.

WILLIAM EXLEY
William is an illustrator living in Southeast London. When not illustrating Explorer books he also works on comics. Will's favourite ancient bug is *Aysheaia* from the Cambrian period.

AQUILA NON CAPIT MUSCAS
THE EAGLE DOES NOT CATCH FLIES

MISSION 01  **DINOSAURS!**

MISSION 02  **BUGS!**

MISSION 03 **PLANTS!**

MISSION 04  **MAMMALS!**

Explorer MISSIONS
Find out more at whatonearthbooks.com

INDEX

A
abdomen 8
ants 7, 21, 23, 31
arachnids 7, 9, 10, 11, 12, 13, 21, 25, 31
Archaeopteryx 15
Arthropleura 15
arthropods 6, 7, 8

B
bacteria 26
bees 7, 17, 21, 23, 24, 27, 30
beetles 27, 31, 32
bristletails 16
butterflies 18, 19, 20

C
camouflage 19, 20, 21
caterpillars 18, 19, 29
centipedes 7, 9, 11
chrysalises 18
cicadas 19, 24
cockroaches 14, 15, 22, 33
colonies 23
communication 24, 25
crabs, horseshoe 32
crickets 20
crustaceans 7, 31

D
damselflies 17
Darwin, Charles 29
dragonflies 14, 15, 16, 18

E
earthworms 29
eggs 10, 19, 20, 23
Eophyllium 21
evolution 6, 7, 10, 11, 16, 17, 18, 19, 20, 21, 22, 29, 32
exoskeletons 7, 8, 10, 13
extinction 12, 17
eyes 9

F
fangs 13, 21
firebrats 16
fireflies 19
fleas 26, 29
flies 9, 17, 29
fossils 11, 15, 16

G
grasshoppers *see* locusts

H
Hallucigenia 6
harvestmen 12
heads 8, 9
Hunt Morgan, Thomas 29

I
insects 7, 8, 9, 11, 14, 15, 16–17, 18, 19, 20, 21, 22–23, 24, 25, 26, 27, 29, 30, 31, 32, 33

L
lacewings 20
larvae 18, 19, 23
leaf insects 21
leeches 28
legs 8, 9, 12, 13, 30
Leizu, Empress 28
locusts 31, 33

M
maggots 18
mantises, praying 19
mates 19, 20, 25
mayflies 16
Mazothairos 15
Meganeura 14, 15
Merian, Maria Sibylla 28
metamorphosis 18
millipedes 8, 9, 15
mites 12
mosquitoes 17, 30, 31
moths 8, 17, 20
myriapods 7, 10, 11

N
nests 22–23, 24, 25, 30
nymphs 18

O
Opabinia 6
ovipositors 21

P
predators 6, 11, 13, 19, 20, 21
prey 6, 12, 13, 20, 21, 25
Pulmonoscorpius 13
pupae 18

R
Rhyniognatha 11
Rothschild, Miriam 29

S
scorpionflies 18, 19
scorpions 9, 13
segments 8
silkworms 28
silverfish 16
spiders 7, 9, 13, 19, 21, 25, 31
spiracles 14
stick insects 21
stingers 21, 23
Sushruta 28

T
tarantulas 21, 31
termites 22–23, 25, 31
thorax 8, 9
ticks 12
trigonotarbids 12
trilobites 6

V
venom 13, 21, 23

W
wasps 7, 19, 21, 23
webs 12, 13, 20, 25
webspinners 20
weevils 9, 32
wings 8, 9, 16–17, 18, 19, 20
woodlice 7, 8, 31
worms 7, 10

THE BUG TIMELINE

We've made it back to the library! Time to look over our findings. Unfold the epic Timeline that traces the entire history of bug life, showcasing 100 different species. Can you find a 'crab' that isn't really a crab? A vinegar spraying scorpion? Or a beetle that people believed made the sun rise in the morning?

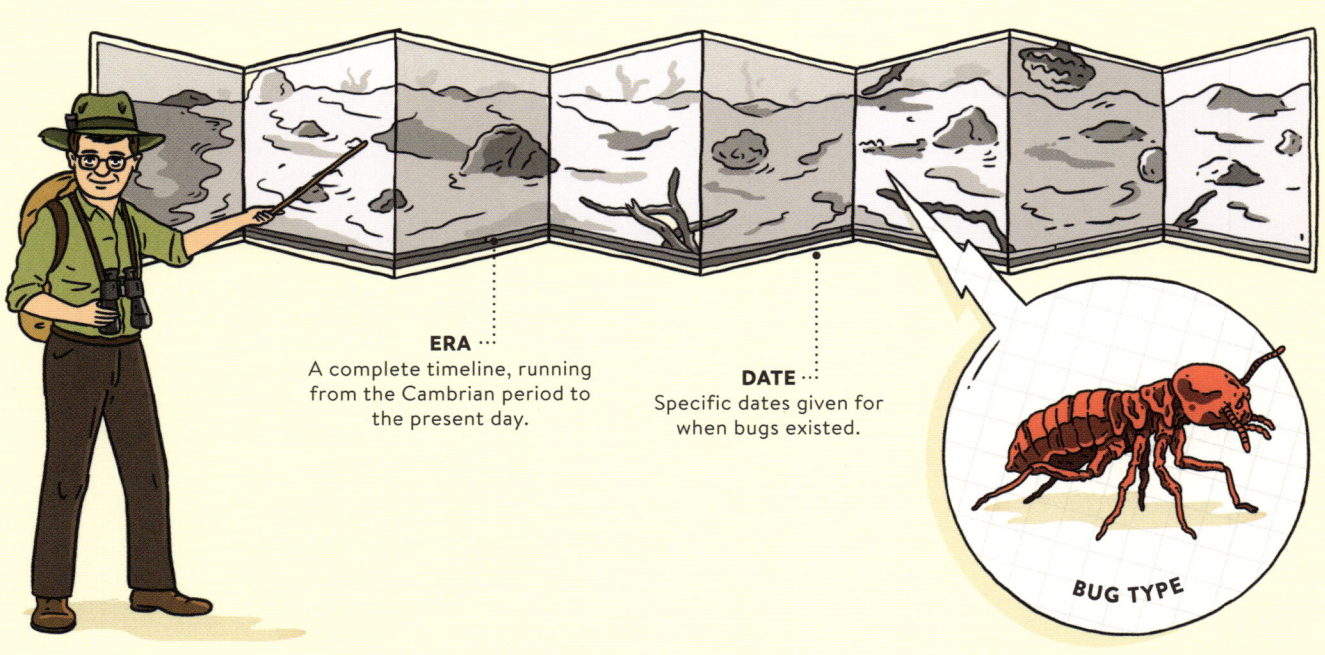

ERA
A complete timeline, running from the Cambrian period to the present day.

DATE
Specific dates given for when bugs existed.

BUG TYPE

EXPLORER BUGS!

515 – LEANCHOILIA
This species used its long, wiry appendages to locate and lasso its prey.

505 – OPABINIA
This five-eyed predator snagged its food with its flexible head-claw.

450 – RAMPHOPRION
This segmented worm lived at sea but over time, its relatives started to live on land. It is a distant relation of a creature commonly found today, the earthworm.

415 – PREARCT[...]
This enormous, clawed, 1m-long [...] hunted prey wit[h] venomous sting[...] the end of its ta[...]

505 – AYSHEAIA
An ancient relative of the velvet worm. Similar species may have been among the first to wriggle out of the sea, on to the land, many millions of years ago.

480 – AEGIROCASSIS
Growing up to 2 metres in length, *Aegirocassis* was a large predator that swam through the seas, on the hunt for other marine life to feed on.

436 – CONCAVICARIS
This species paddled through the seas using its oar-shaped rear limbs. Its group died out entirely millions of years ago.

428 – ERAMOSCORPIUS
This nimble predator was an ea[rly] type of scorpion. It would have lived mostly underwater, but its feet suggest it also came on to land.

505 – HALLUCIGENIA
This species' long spiky body deterred attacks from predators. Its shape was confusing at first, until scientists realised they had reconstructed it upside down.

445 – LUNATASPIS
Although known as 'horseshoe crabs', *Lunataspis* was from a group of arachnids more closely related to scorpions and spiders than crabs.

450 – SCOYENIA
Tiny tunnels preserved in the landscape provide the only evidence of one of the first species to crawl out of the sea and survive on dry land. It was probably similar to a millipede today.

427 – PNEUM[...]
This millipede's [...] enabled it to ta[ke] the air, an ada[ptation] it could survive[...]

520 – HUPETINA
The tough external armour of these trilobites would have protected them from predators. Trilobites died out in a mass extinction 252 million years ago.

495 – CAMBROPYCNOGON
This ancient sea spider, the oldest yet discovered, is not classed as a spider or even an arachnid, but rather another form of life entirely. Some sea spiders live thousands of metres below the sea surface.

422 – PALAEOTARBUS
This trigonotarbid had eight legs just like a spider, but un[like] a spider, it didn't produce silk or weave any webs.

CAMBRIAN PERIOD	ORDOVICIAN PERIOD	SILURIAN PERIOD
520 Million years ago	480	440

Rhyniognatha – 412 million years ago

Meganeura – 300 million years ago

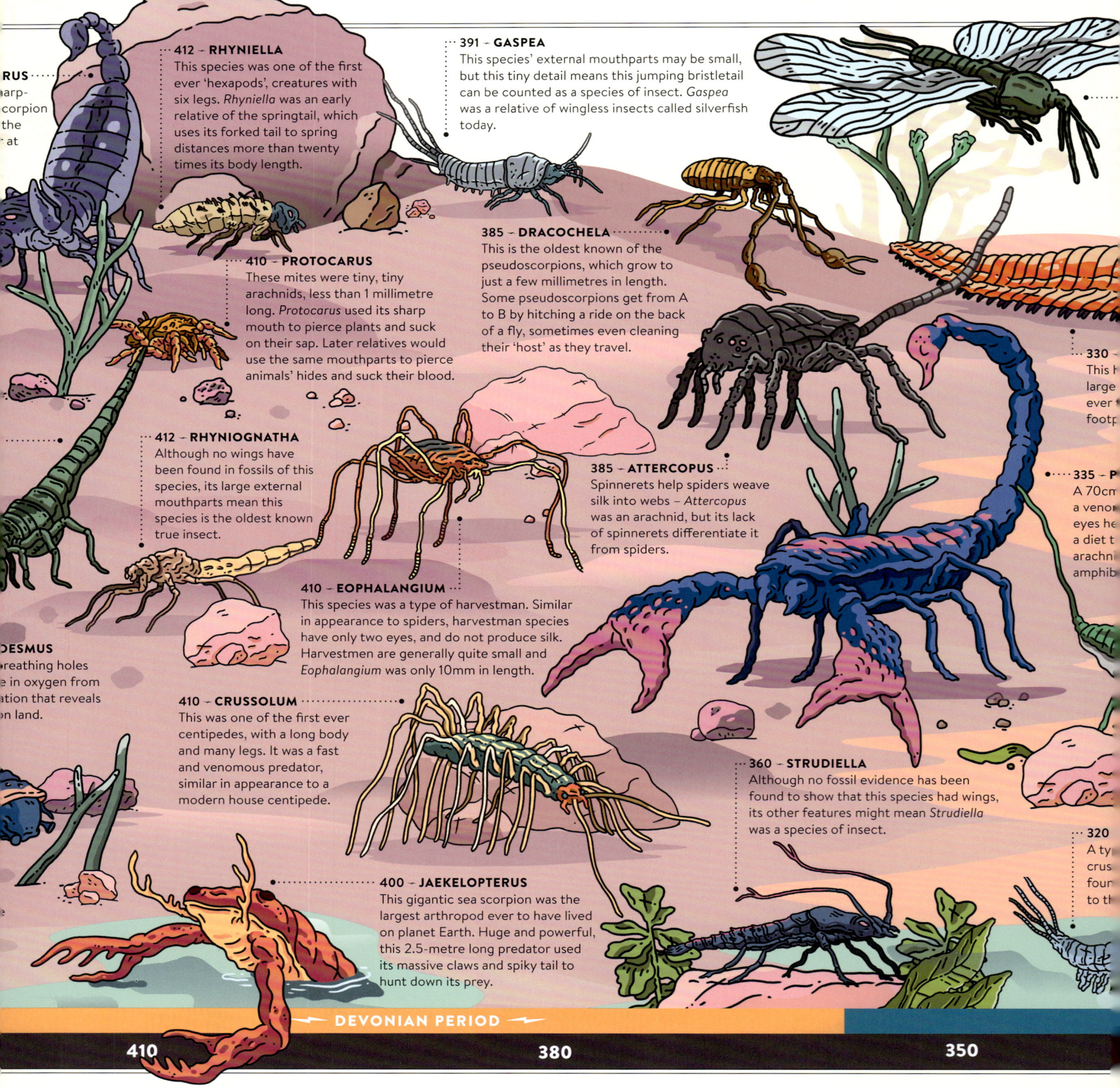

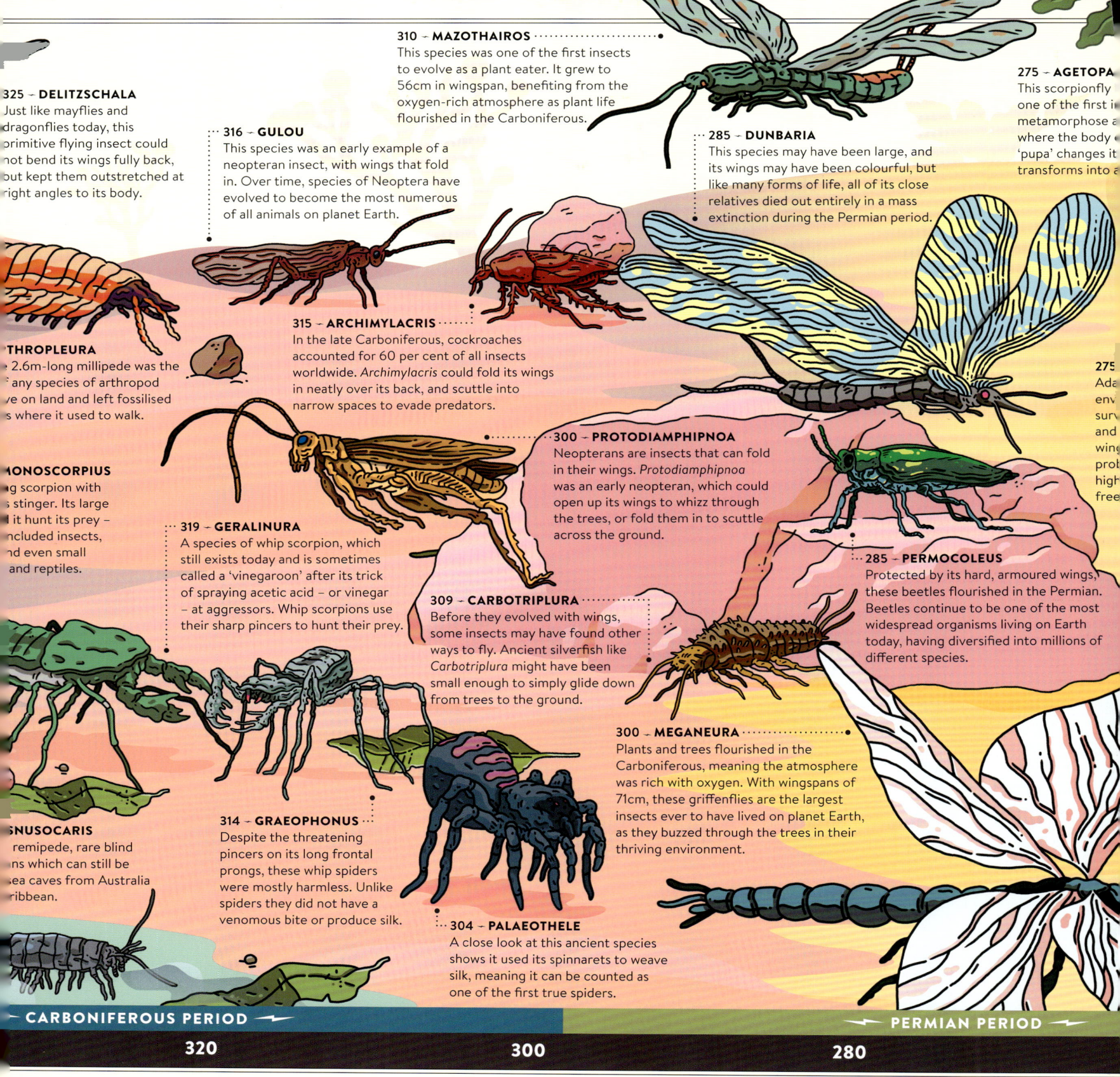

Pulmonoscorpius – 335 million years ago

Eophalangium – 410 million years ago

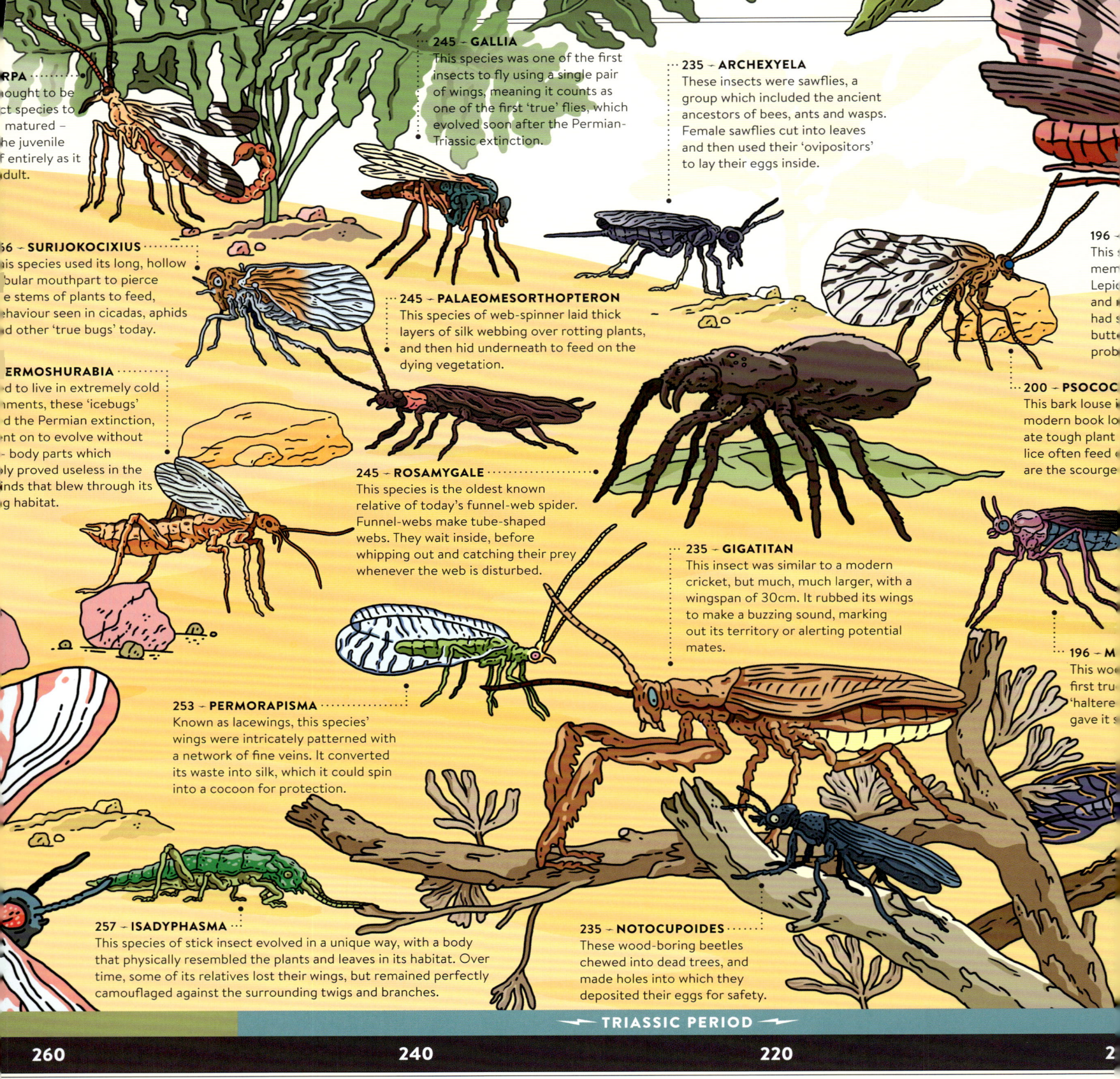

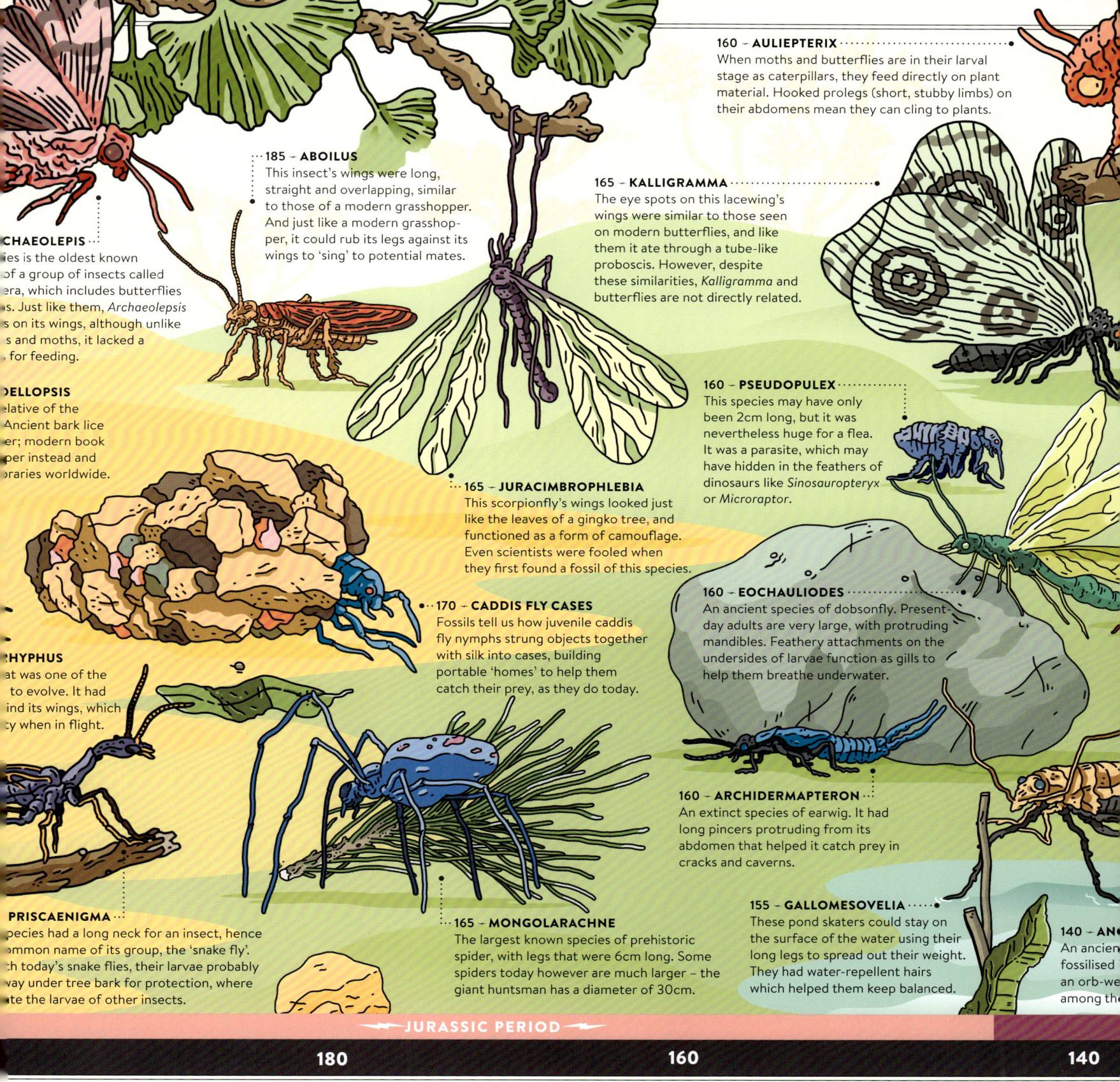

Auliepterix – 160 million years ago

Paleoculis - 75 million years ago

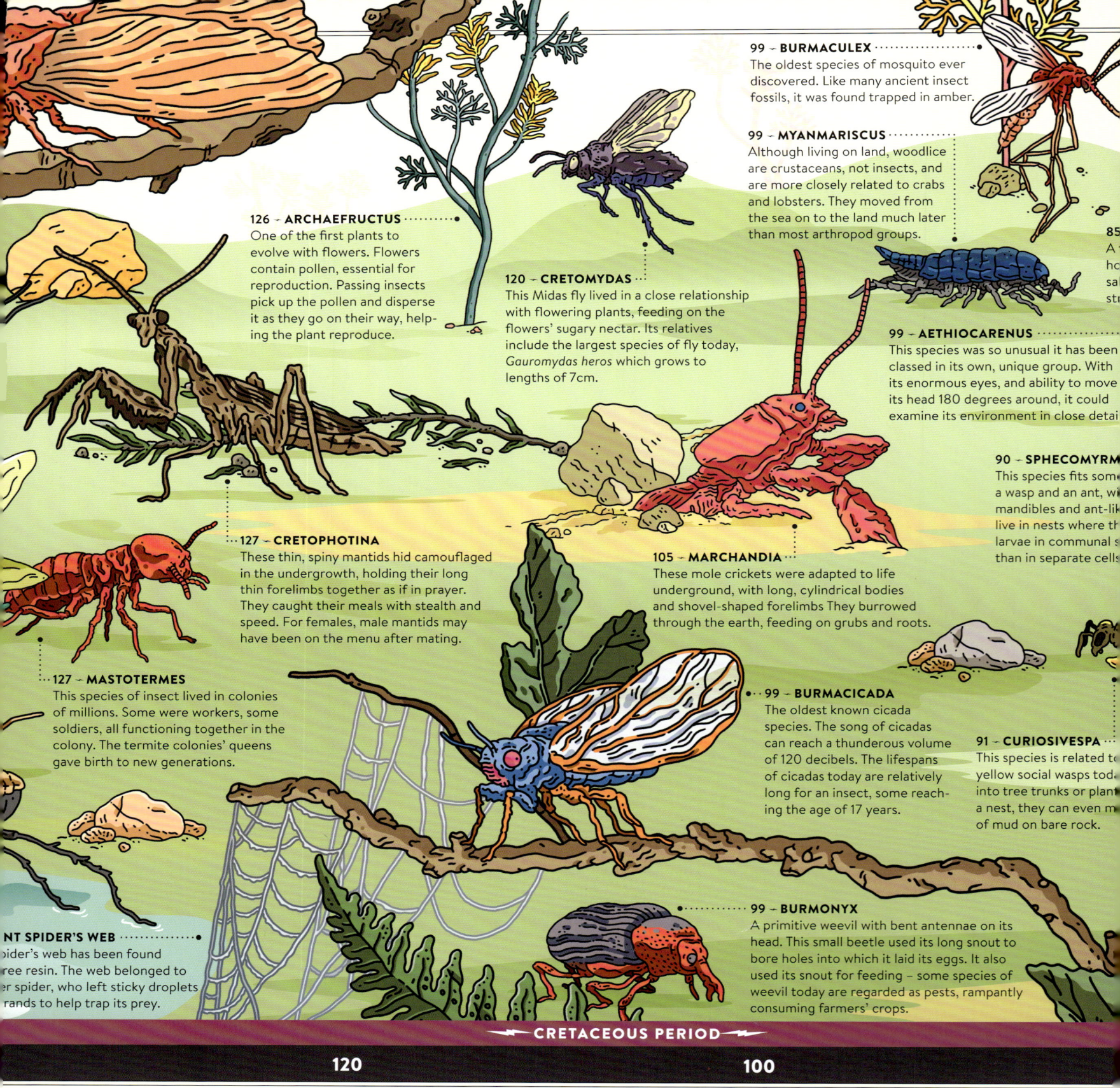

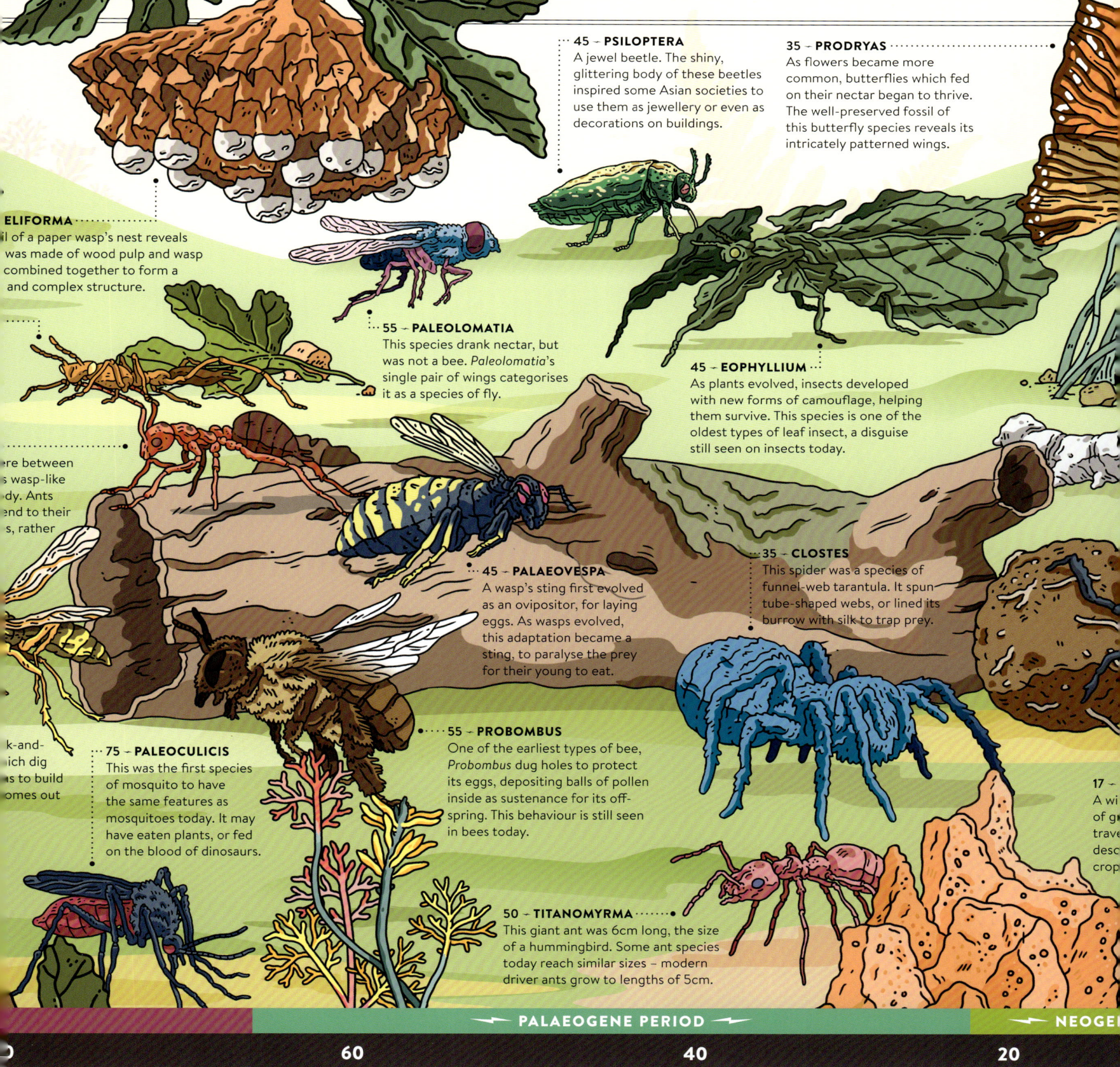

Pneumodesmus - 427 million years ago

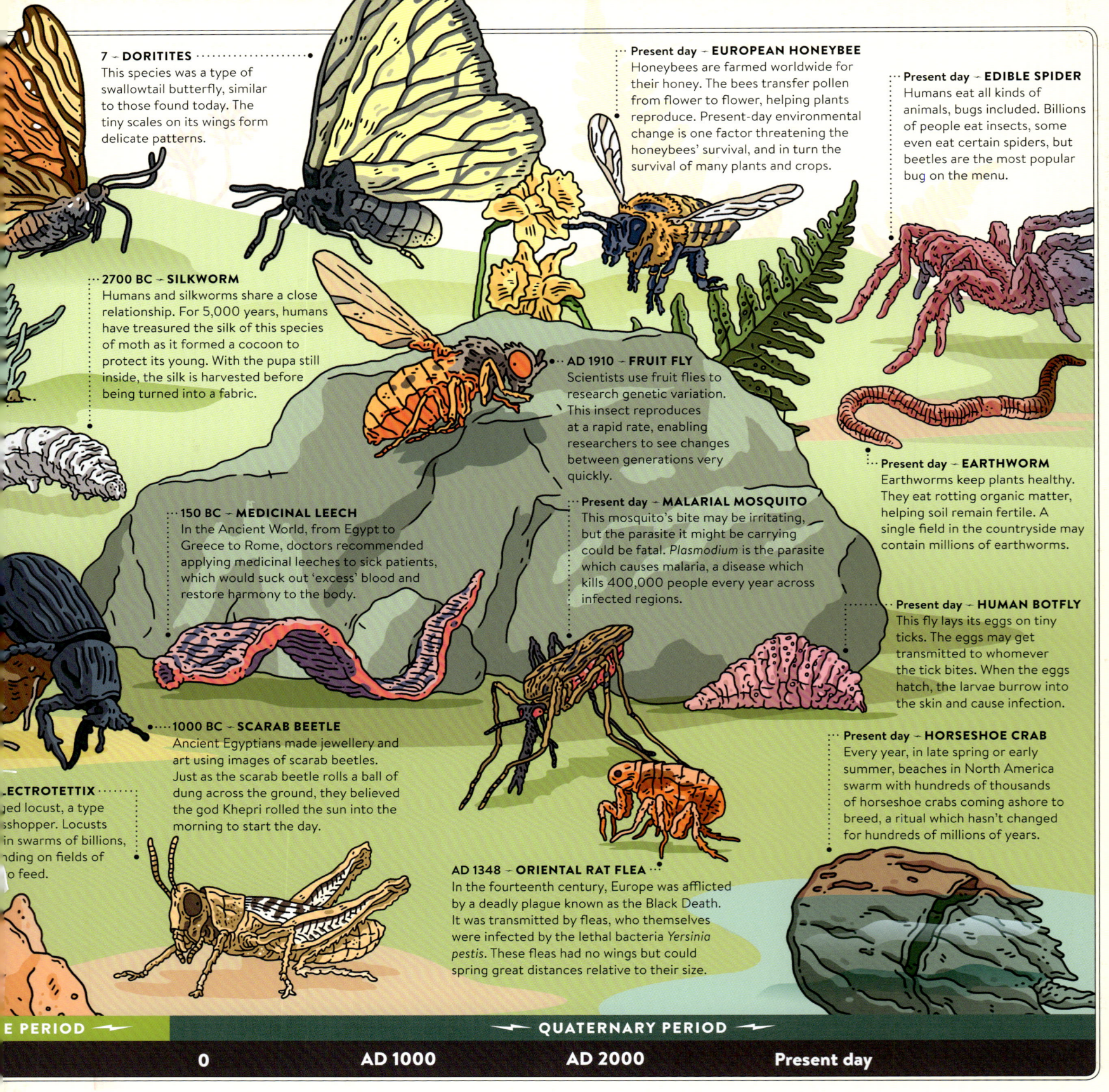